God's presence is evident in the life of Ms. Von Bruck. More than just a heartwarming story, this work is spiritually stirring . . . marvelously refreshing!

—TED HAGGARD
SENIOR PASTOR, NEW LIFE CHURCH
COLORADO SPRINGS, COLORADO

This book is a celebration of the grace and mercy of God as our faithful Guide and constant Protector. You will be inspired to trust the Lord with your future, as His destiny for your life unfolds step by step. This is a must read!

—ROBERT STEARNS
EXECUTIVE DIRECTOR, EAGLES WINGS MINISTRIES
NEW YORK, NEW YORK

Voyage is inspiring and encouraging! May all of God's children discover that we are on a voyage to eternal glory. The grace of God is the ship that carries us, the water on which we sail and the wind that drives us to the Father.

—DR. RON CREWS
PRESIDENT, MASSACHUSETTS FAMILY INSTITUTE
NEWTON, MASSACHUSETTS

This is an extraordinary story of God's grace—reaching both the mountain tops and the valleys of life. This story will encourage every reader to see God's presence throughout the journey of life.

—JOSEPH M. FORD
SENIOR PASTOR, CALVARY TEMPLE
HOLDEN, MASSACHUSETTS

Voyage is good reading! It is a well-written message for our day, when people need to build intimacy with God by really knowing Him—His character, His plans and, mostly, His heart!

—RUTH HICKMAN
FOUNDER AND TEACHER, ABUNDANT WORD MINISTRIES
LAKEWOOD, COLORADO

Edeltraud Von Bruck has seen God perform the miraculous! But this is more than an amazing true story; it is a testimony to the vastness of the Father's love and desire toward us. We are clearly shown the exciting life we can have if we are prepared to listen and respond to God's voice.

—ANDY WOODWARD
SENIOR PASTOR, NEW LIFE CHRISTIAN FELLOWSHIP
WEST COWES, ENGLAND

Voyage will enrich your soul and refresh your spirit! Von Bruck's journey is full of experiences of the grace of God and insights into how to walk in His Spirit day by day.

—DR. RICHARD A. GERMAINE
SENIOR PASTOR, FIRST CONGREGATIONAL CHURCH
HOPKINTON, MASSACHUSETTS

Here is the unique story of one woman's journey. Her vivid descriptions of life's perilous voyage stir the poet within me. And my soul is encouraged by the reminder that God is always with us, even in the most difficult of times, to "set our shipwrecked souls a'sail again."

—DONNA KRIEGER
COMPOSER, CONCERT AND RECORDING ARTIST, POET, TEACHER
NORTH KINGSTOWN, RHODE ISLAND

My prayer is that this work of timely revelation and prophetic insight may catch the sails of many lost at sea. And may it inspire us to "offer ourselves to be instruments of His hand to rescue and to enable others to embark upon the voyage ordained by His grace. Let us help them to reach the Rock of Ages, to enter the harbor of God's presence and to partake of the treasures of God's kingdom."

—NAN CONNOR
PROPHETIC INTERCESSOR AND LAY MINISTER
BEL AIR, MARYLAND

The Journey to Eternal Glory

Voyage

E. VON BRUCK

CREATION
HOUSE
PRESS

VOYAGE: THE JOURNEY TO ETERNAL GLORY by E. Von Bruck
Published by Creation House Press
A part of Strang Communications Company
600 Rinehart Road
Lake Mary, Florida 32746
www.creationhouse.com

Unless otherwise noted, all Scripture quotations are from the New King James Version of the Bible. Copyright © 1979, 1980, 1982, 1984 by Thomas Nelson, Inc., publishers. Used by permission.

Library of Congress Control Number: 2001096409
International Standard Book Number: 0-88419-825-1

01 02 03 04 8 7 6 5 4 3 2 1
Printed in the United States of America

ACKNOWLEDGMENTS

MY GRATITUDE EXTENDS to the many people who were willing to be instruments of God's love and compassion in my life. First, I thank my parents (now departed from this earth to reside in heavenly places) who labored to raise a family with great enthusiasm and who set an inspiring example to minister the gospel in word and in deed to many people, sometimes with great sacrifice. Special thanks are given to my friend Lorraine Gutowsky who, at a most difficult time in my life, patiently extended her helping heart and hand. Deep appreciation is extended to Roberta and Thomas Raffa who urged me on to complete the book and seek publication.

Sincere thanks also to Jeanne Price, Mary Rogers, the Uber family, the Perry family, the Willis family and the Meola family for their fellowship and superb hospitality while I taught at various Christian schools. Extra special thanks to James Foley who expertly and diligently typed the entire manuscript. There was one other person who deserves honorable mention but wishes to wait for her reward in heaven. Despite her already very busy schedule, she labored many hours typing the first draft of this book on her laptop computer—sometimes in her cozy living room in front of a fire, another time on the beach in Southern Georgia. Thanks, SCHWESTERLEIN.

CONTENTS

FOREWORD

THIS BOOK IS a personal account of God's perpetual desire to make Himself known to us, to guide us through the valleys and over the mountaintops of everyday life, and to bring us into a significant relationship with Him. It is an acknowledgement of His grace and power which have been evident in my own life as well as in the lives of countless believers around the world. It is a testimony of God's handiwork and the saving, healing and enriching quality of His presence.

Introduction

BORN AND RAISED in Austria, surrounded by a Christian, cultured and educated family, I had the great privilege of growing from a young age in the knowledge of the Lord Jesus Christ. Experiencing first hand God's protection and provision during World War II and later observing the dedication of both my parents to use their talents to minister the Word of God constantly inspired me as a child. (My father was a teacher and Baptist preacher, my mother a singer).

Upon immigrating to the United States and completing a college education in French and Spanish Literature, God led me to use my own gifts and skills to work as a foreign language teacher in various Christian schools—grades kindergarten through college. I also worked as a counselor in children's institutions and as a governess and tutor in private homes. Apart from my working endeavors, I was involved with lay counseling within the local church and music ministry—I have composed over two hundred sacred songs.

Despite some extraordinary experiences within everyday living as well as with my relationship with God, I have, at times, witnessed great hardship, both physically and emotionally. However, the hand of God always reached down to restore and deliver and, in the process, to deepen my relationship with Him.

It is now my prayer that by these chapters I have an opportunity to pass on the hope for comfort, salvation and restoration that is available to us in Christ Jesus. It is also my heart's cry to challenge the reader to seek God's presence and a personal relationship with Him who seeks to abide in us.

—E. VON BRUCK

PART I

VOYAGE ORDAINED BY GRACE

CHAPTER 1

RAGING STORM

I T WAS JUNE, 1956. I was about fourteen, crossing the Atlantic with my parents and younger sister on the way to Europe, the cradle of my childhood. The ocean liner was being bounced around by four-story high waves spilling their foamy ocean sprays like torrents onto the front decks. The bow of the ship pierced and dipped deeply into the monstrous waters, then came up for air, repeating this cycle all through the night. We were in the middle of a hurricane.

As the boat was tossed to and fro in the violent winds, our hearts and minds were forced into a turbulent journey with the threat of perishing lurking behind the howling winds. Many a passenger, no doubt, bargained with God that brutal night, in the hope of gaining His protection and favor.

Everyone on the ship was seasick, including myself. Hoping it would help to get some fresh air, I foolishly stepped onto the middle bar of the deck's railing and bent over to deposit my "dinner" into the sea. In the fury of the winds, I momentarily lost my balance and anticipated that the deep, dark ocean was going to swallow me up. With utmost precision of timing, I felt a hand pulling me back to safety.

I turned around but there was no one there.

In all the years ahead I would wonder why God would care enough to stretch out His hand to rescue me at that crucial

1

moment in my life. It was one instant in one child's life that reflected God's unending desire to deliver mankind from tumbling into the deep sea of despair and to bring us safely back into His presence. It was one moment that reflected His passion to save us and to take us on a voyage, ordained by His grace, from the kingdom of darkness, defeat and death to His kingdom of eternal life, triumph and glory.

> The floods have lifted up, O Lord,
> The floods have lifted up their voice;
> The floods lift up their waves.
> The Lord on high is mightier
> Than the noise of many waters,
> Than the mighty waves of the sea.
> —Psalm 93:3-4

> For so an entrance will be supplied to you abundantly into the everlasting kingdom of our Lord and Savior Jesus Christ.
> —2 Peter 1:11

> And this is eternal life, that they may know You, the only true God, and Jesus Christ whom You have sent.
> —John 17:3

> But may the God of all grace, who called us to His eternal glory by Christ Jesus, after you have suffered a while, perfect, establish, strengthen and settle you.
> —1 Peter 5:10

Two days later, a number of early risers waited for the sun to emerge from the now crystal clear, still waters of sapphire blue. I decided to join them. Twenty minutes after the captain's designated time of sunrise, this ball of fire, the center of our solar system that sustains life on our planet, had seemingly still refused to pay its regular visit. I almost panicked at the thought of a dreadful verdict of nature's imminent extinction. However, my sister came running like a messenger of hope,

"Come, see the gorgeous sunrise!" she called.

My heart leaped and I shouted, "Where? Where?"

"At the back of the ship!" she replied hurriedly.

I followed her, then stood somewhat bewildered but in awe at the sight of a crimson sun bathed in a scarlet sky and sea. Soon, everyone on board recovered from the unsettling question, "Why isn't the sun rising?"

As it turned out, the captain had turned the ship around during the night to pick up a severely injured passenger from a freighter that couldn't offer sufficient medical care. Those who remained on deck watched the approach of the freighter from beyond the horizon. First we could only see its puffs of smoke, then its chimneys and finally the entire ship. Eventually it greeted us with low tooting sounds. The patient was transferred in a life-boat and successfully cared for while our ship, like a fat whale, labored to make a 180 degree turn to face the east again to resume its original course toward the European shores.

The next few days were glorious and luxurious. This time the ship sailed like a swan in a glistening bowl of emerald green as the sun mesmerized those aboard. My sister and I, like young detectives, watched a number of soap operas develop among some adults. Each person on this voyage traveled for a different reason; each one told a different life's story that could have, perhaps, ended in the fierce storm. But each one of our lives was steered ahead again in full force.

For entertainment and recreation there were swimming pools, ping-pong tables, concert halls, dance halls and a movie-theater. We indulged in fancy food served in various opulent dining halls by elegant waiters. One of them had carried a stack of thirty plates from the kitchen only to watch them lean like the Tower of Pisa and tumble hopelessly to the floor, crashing violently in a chorus of dissonant sounds. The whole process seemed intriguing to me, especially watching the expressions on the poor waiter's face.

3

All heavy furniture like dining tables, benches and lounge chairs had been put back in place after they had tumbled from one side of the ship to the other during its sways across ominous waves during the previous night of terror. Now that the sea was tame again, the ship carried us like a cradle ever so gently swinging in a mother's arms. Our hearts cooed like little children in a play-pen, totally carefree for the moment. It was indeed the first day of the rest of our lives.

CHAPTER 2

BACK TO THE ROOTS

ONLY TEN MONTHS prior to this tumultuous ocean voyage my family, including my two older sisters, had emigrated from Austria to the United States. On the day of our departure from our homeland my heart had been torn apart, as our train pulled away leaving friends and extended family behind to disappear in the distance. Among them was my aging grandmother, a poet, who had written each one of us girls an endearing farewell poem. She stood there, brave as could be, waving with one hand, blessing us with the other, reaching to touch our hearts one more time.

In order to soothe my agonizing emotions, I thought of the exciting adventure awaiting me and my family in America, the land of the free. Somehow I pictured Indians and wild animals, even lions, roaming the terrain of the New World.

After a night-long train ride, we embarked on a Dutch ocean-liner to cross the Atlantic Ocean for the first time in our lives. It took fourteen days to reach the shores of North America. I had never before appreciated the sight of land as much as on that day of arrival. Moreover, my excitement grew far beyond my expectations when I first glanced at the elegant Statue of Liberty welcoming us as we entered the New York harbor. Within an hour our ship was face to face with the foreboding mass of concrete skyscrapers of New York City. My heart trembled at this sight. It was to me as if I were facing an impenetrable monster. My shock subsided, however, when I realized that there were only people living and working in these gigantic buildings. Upon setting foot on the piers of New York, my parents stood there in brave anticipation with four children by their side, sixteen boxes of personal belongings and five dollars in their pockets.

My mother, not knowing any English and missing her home and friends back in Austria, cried for hours in the ensuing weeks. My father found no work due to lingering discrimination towards German speaking people, the wounds of World War II not having healed and the winds of the Cold War between the United States and German allies not having been totally calmed. After laboring to survive the first ten months in the New World, my parents decided to return to our homeland with my younger sister and me, leaving behind my two older sisters who were old enough to be employed. They had found employment in Elizabeth, New Jersey. In the meantime, my parents, my younger sister and I set foot again on the European continent that had kept our roots alive and welcomed us back with open arms. My torn heart was mending as I again embraced my grandmother, my aunts and uncles and old friends. Even familiar mountains, towns and lakes seemed to welcome us back. For a while we took residency in a farmhouse at the edge of a crystal clear lake called Attersee. We had spent summers at that lake during my childhood. Within a few weeks its surrounding pastures, hills and sheltering mountain peaks were dusted with early autumn snow.

To get to school each day, my sister and I had to take a ferryboat across this lake, then ride on an old steam engine train. After the third stop, we still had to walk twenty minutes to get to school. Those were the most memorable school days of my life. Before we headed out on this extensive journey to school each day, my mother heated fresh cow's milk on a wood-burning stove. At six in the morning the baker's son would bring freshly baked rolls that spread a heartwarming aroma through the entire house. Occasionally, the one milk-producing cow that lived in the barn attached to the house would bellow approvingly, making its presence known to early risers and still slumbering residents.

By October, the foliage on the hills had turned brilliant colors, barely brushed by a whisper of frost and snow, leaving a vibrant reflection in the deep crystal waters of the lake. The lake had served pre-historic, stilt-building people thousands of years ago, and to this day it inspires countless painters and vacationers from many lands. My mother periodically visited her friend Anni v. Clanner, an academic portrait painter, who lived across the lake. She would also visit her singing instructor, Dr. Iro, who coached her in the art of opera and German Lieder, a repertoire of classical songs. It was, for us, a time of intimacy and re-bonding with family and bosom friends, as well as a time to breathe in deeply the fragrances of the homeland and absorb its rich culture once again.

However, just before Christmas, my sweet homeland was awakened cruelly by the shocking news of the Communist invasion of Hungary. Located right next to Austria, Hungary, once part of an extensive Austrian Empire, now had become a vicious threat to its neighboring lands. Fearing a Communist takeover of Austria, my parents decided to rush back to the United States. We packed our bags, celebrated Christmas with my grandmother and bid her good-bye. My heart was grieving once again, as the train fled silently through exquisite, snowy countryside in the dusk of Christmas Day.

As snow flakes danced by the train windows, episodes of my childhood passed through my mind, as if to make a final imprint on my heart. My first recollection was my mother's face frowning in horror as she viewed her bedroom mirror shattered by flying pieces of bombs during World War II. During another bombing raid, our nanny had been blown to bits on a bridge while walking home carrying a bucket of fresh milk for us kids. We then moved to another town, but the bombing followed us there. I remembered hiding in the dark basement during air raids, the children screaming and our parents praying day and night. When it was all over, every house around us had been hit; some were left in total shambles. Our place alone stood unscathed. During the aftermath of the war, I spent countless hours crying, contemplating what it must be like to die while buried under the rubble of a house demolished by bombings. I was only three years of age and couldn't verbalize my agonizing preoccupation with death and dying. Later, when I went to school, I heard war stories over and over again. That is how society deals with the trauma and the devastating effects of war.

Occasionally I would see dolls or toys peeking out from under the rubble of neighborhood houses ripped apart by war. And I would shudder to think a child might have died under there. To make matters worse, we were continually hungry. Food was not readily available, and often we lived on coffee and cornmeal or cabbage for days or weeks on end. We had meat once or twice a year. I had my first ice cream cone when I was ten years old, when things were better and much restoration had occurred.

After the war had ended, my father was gone a lot. He would bicycle miles, sometimes in freezing rain or even snow, to nearby towns, to preach the gospel and hold Bible studies, as he had done underground during the Nazi occupation of Austria. During that time he could have been convicted and possibly executed for religious anti-Nazi activity alongside six million Jews and twelve million non-Jews, many of them Christians. My father had almost been drafted into the Nazi army. At one point he was almost sent to join the troops attacking Russia, where 85 percent of the German army either bled, starved or froze to death. But two hours before his departure,

8

my dad came down with a 104-degree fever. He was considered unfit and was sent home, escaping the bloody battlefields and the torturous arctic weather of Russia. Later on, until the end of the war, my father was stationed at a comparatively easy post as a military weatherman. God had spared his life for a reason. Throughout my childhood I was in awe of my mother's fervent prayers. God's sovereign protection of my dad—as well as of my maternal grandfather, who, during World War I, also had barely escaped death while imprisoned in a Siberian labor camp for several years—left a deep impression on my young heart concerning the power of prayer.

In his boyhood, my father had experienced the traumatic effects of World War I, as well as abuse and abandonment by his brilliant but alcoholic father, a college professor at the University of Prague. My father's search for God and his newly found Christian faith during his young adult years led to a call and commitment to preach the gospel, the good news of Jesus Christ. After World War II, during the many years of our country's restoration from the devastation of war, my father converted an old truck into a vehicle from which a huge tent could be unfolded and used for evangelistic services. Many people were hungry for God and desperate for hope and peace, but the government and general public did not welcome such an unconventional display of Christian service. Thus, my father's tent services were considered quite an oddity in our community. In my heart I felt embarrassed at first, but after some struggle I made a firm decision to honor, at any price, the message of the resurrection power of Jesus Christ who bore our sins on the cross. He is, after all, the only answer to man's dilemma caused by separation from God—the only reconciling factor between God and man.

How privileged I felt to have received this good news of God's love and of the price His Son Jesus paid on the cross as a ransom for my sin. I also felt exceedingly privileged to have

9

found eternal life and God's presence in my soul. It was my mother who, upon my request at age seven, had instructed me to take Jesus into my heart in order to receive life everlasting. Remembering the agonizing hours of my young childhood spent attempting to come to grips with death, my whole soul silently screamed to know this Giver of Life. After we prayed, I hesitated, wondering in anguish who this Jesus really was. At that moment, I saw Jesus appear, brighter than the sun, purer than snow and more glorious than silver or gold. I knew instantly that He was the Son of God—powerful, but harmless, innocent and pure, one in whom I could hope and trust.

In the sight of His brightness and righteousness, I felt sin in my heart. I repented and accepted His forgiveness and cleansing presence in my heart and soul. This episode totally changed my attitude towards life and death. My unspeakable gratitude for having found the true fountain of life in the midst of worldwide tragedy and death birthed within me the desire to mirror the Light of God and His Son Jesus wherever I would go.

Reminiscing about these sacred moments in the ensuing years was like drawing hope and strength from a well that would never go dry. Whenever I nearly fainted in the presence of tragedy and despair, God would refresh me with a drink from His well, the fountain of Living Water that flows from the throne of God the Father and His Son Jesus Christ.

As the train sped away into the night, I also pondered our family unity and cultural heritage which would later greatly enhance our family's life in the United States. Endearing memories of my parents' sacrifices for my valuable and treasured exposure to the arts lingered in my heart that night and in many years to come. One Christmas, to my surprise, my mother had bought me ice skates and ballet shoes. Another Christmas, my father acquired my much desired violin—I had hoped to gain the attention of a boy who also played the violin. Eventually, my mother arranged for me to have piano, violin and ballet lessons, none of which we could afford.

I composed my first piano piece at age ten or twelve, and our house was a continual concert hall of music, poetry and dance. My father's uncle was Austrian literary poet Heinrich Gartner. My mother and my father's two brothers were opera singers, and my sisters all played the piano. We spent holidays enjoying an array of family performances. We passed summer nights on pristine lakeshores, softly singing hymns and Alpine folk songs like nightingales in the evening breeze. As swans glided along the shimmering lake and as evening lights reflected and danced in the water like jewels in a midnight mirror, we would reaffirm our unspoken love for one another and our commitment to God and to our family unity.

These treasures of our heritage greatly enriched the life of my family and enabled us to contribute to our new community in the United States.

Chapter 3

Reunion

On January 4, 1957, my parents, my younger sister and I returned to the United States. My two older sisters awaited our arrival eagerly, and the joy of our reunion was profound. We celebrated Christmas for the next three days in front of a voluptuous Christmas tree laden with lights and accompanied by a mountain of presents. The thankfulness we felt about being together surpassed our excitement of comparative material wealth exhibited during this festive holiday. As usual, my father read the Christmas story from his Bible, and we all prayed and thanked God for safely reuniting us. We also thanked God for enabling us to pray, worship and celebrate *Him* freely in a nation under God.

With newly found hope for a blessed future, our family embarked on a new year and on a journey into the unknown with God at our side and a song in our hearts—"Let freedom ring!" We eagerly anticipated a life of freedom from threats of war; freedom from hunger and despair; freedom from pain and persecution and freedom from deprivation and fear. *God bless America!*

One Sunday afternoon, we searched for things to do. We realized more than ever that we had left all our friends and extended family behind. In searching for something or someone familiar to connect with, my mother mentioned that her great-aunt had visited Texas in the early 1900's. Just for the fun of it and expressing the secret hope we all had of finding someone related to us in this country, we opened a huge New York City phone book to look for this lady's name. When we actually found her name, we all gasped. Could it really be the same person? When one of us dialed the number, an elderly lady with an Austrian accent answered. Our hearts beat faster. Upon a thorough exchange of information regarding family trees and bits and pieces of long lost family stories, we realized that she was indeed our relative. She was already in her eighties. We were ecstatic to have found such an unexpected treasure. With great anticipation, we appointed a time to meet with her.

Tante Relly, as we called her, had come by boat to this country in the early 1900's. She had missed getting on the Titanic by about twenty people. Many hundreds had been on the waiting list to take this extraordinary luxury liner on its maiden voyage.

She also informed us that she had a daughter, a sister, a niece and some grandchildren. Her niece was married to a naval officer active in the medical field. He was on board a ship stationed in Newport, Rhode Island. On a beautiful summer weekend we drove to Newport to meet our newly found cousin and her family. Since my English was scarce, my conversation with our cousins was at a minimum. I excused myself and wandered around the neighborhood. Within minutes I came to a path along the shore only to fall in love with the ocean breeze, the rose-hemmed cliffs on one side of the ocean walk and manicured lawns surrounding the gigantic mansions on the other. Early morning rays shimmered in the waves that rolled like silver ribbons towards the shore. Seagulls spread their wings to sail in the wind while flocks of other birds choreographed their dances in the air. In the distance, sailboats, like a parade of white swans, were gliding in the ocean mists. I was mesmerized by the pristine beauty of this place. I knew our family could be happy here, and I couldn't bear the thought of leaving.

Back at the house I asked for a phone book and, in broken English, called several schools asking (on my dad's behalf) if they might need a German teacher. I feared they would misinterpret my intentions for a prank call and would hang up on me, but to my surprise, one schoolmaster replied, "We don't need one but we could introduce German classes. Send him right over." When I excitedly related this to my dad, he thought I was making a joke, so I called the school back and let my father talk to the director himself. Within that hour my dad was hired as teacher of German, math and physics in a private high school for millionaires' boys. It consisted of a gigantic castle by the sea and several other mansions for dormitories. We were accommodated in the charming coach house of one of the mansions and had the privilege of joining staff and students for their formal Sunday dinners. My mother acquired a piano for us girls to practice on. Soon she supplied us with a new piano teacher and herself with a pianist in order to pursue her singing endeavors. Eventually she would give concerts in some of the mansions by the sea, and at times, incorporated us girls into her program. By then we had developed into semi-accomplished classical pianists.

My father eventually held German Bible studies in our home and occasionally preached in the local Baptist Church. My two older sisters had married and often visited, especially when it was time to introduce us to their newborns. That was always a grand occasion to celebrate.

We spent summer vacations basking in the sun on pebbled and sandy beaches. We enjoyed listening to the lulling sounds of the sea, to seagull tunes and to the orchestra of ocean waves crashing against steadfast rocks that guarded the shoreline with dignified authority from the high tides of the sea. My dad would sail all day while my mother sang into the sun. My sister and I would swim to little rocks and islands, mastering the water's currents, tides and forbidding waves that rose above us and spilled over like liquid emerald curtains, descending with magnificent force. We learned to respect the power of the sea.

In 1957, on America's birthday, we joined Newport residents in celebrating the Fourth of July. The day was celebrated by watching old-fashioned parades in the morning and listening to piccolos and drums playing American tunes. In the evening we joined the crowds gasping in awe as the brilliant colors of fireworks reflected in the sea like dancing fire. It was our first Fourth of July celebration.

Being immersed in this idyllic environment helped us heal from the ravages of war. The cultural ambiance of Newport was also a comfort and a constant source of inspiration to further develop our musical talents and to share them with the community. Concerts were hosted in the various mansions, where the public could also enjoy seeing many exquisite artifacts. Some evenings, my younger sister and I volunteered to hand out concert programs at entrance doors. The ladies wore long evening gowns that swayed in the gentle ocean breeze, and fragrances of freshly watered rose gardens tickled our romantic fantasies.

One night, Miss Schweitzer, a renowned European pianist and sister of Dr. Albert Schweitzer, gave a concert. It was an evening to remember. Little did I know that the next day she would be one of the judges at the Miss Newport contest, in which I was a contestant. Only minutes before I went on stage, someone told me about Miss Schweitzer's presence as one of the judges. I was stunned, since I had coincidentally elected to play one of the same piano pieces Miss Schweitzer had so brilliantly performed the night before. I considered withdrawing from the contest, but my best friend, who was a contestant as well, urged me to stay as moral support for her throughout this ordeal. Since her father was dying of cancer, my compassion for her was greater than my fear. I marched bravely on stage to play. My friend won the title of Miss Newport and continued in the Miss America pageant. I was first runner-up and was very happy for my friend who needed and deserved the crown.

On other memorable occasions, I would walk to town to watch Jack and Jackie Kennedy exit the Catholic Church after Sunday mass. My piano teacher, Mrs. Marion Van Slyke, frequently accompanied singers who were invited to perform at Jackie's childhood summer home, The Hammersmith Farm. Many years later she played the organ at Jackie Kennedy's mother's memorial service.

I studied French, math and Spanish at a Catholic college a few blocks from our home. The school was housed in an enormous French Huguenot castle overlooking the sea. Its main hall had marble floors, gilded stairways and magnificent murals on a four-story high ceiling. The fairy tale atmosphere made it hard for me to concentrate on my studies at times.

During my graduation ball, the dance floor was extended through opened tall glass doors framed with velvet curtains into a large marble deck lined with classic stone banisters. The soft pounding of ocean waves in the distance accompanied the melodious rhythms of the elegant graduation dance. Surrounding the magnificent architecture were formal gardens and walkways laced with beds of roses that sweetly enhanced the invigorating fragrances of the sea.

My personal acquaintance with one of the professors there, a grandson of an American literary poet, was a highlight of my studies there. We both loved God and implemented our artistic abilities for His glory.

To my great joy, the school had Maria Van Trapp as special speaker one day. She was the real-life lady portrayed in the film *The Sound of Music.* It was a thrill to chat with her in German.

She beamed with the love of Jesus. Her family sang like angels, more beautifully than the characters in the movie. Later on, her daughter Rosemarie (born to her and Captain Van Trapp) lived at my sister's house, where we enjoyed singing hymns and Austrian folk songs together.

In Newport, I used to bicycle around our neighborhood. One day, I met a lady with a Polish accent walking a dog. With my own accent I greeted her and asked her where she was from. She spoke fluent German, having fled from Poland during World War II and having lived in Vienna before immigrating to the United States at age seventeen. I introduced her to my mother who promptly and regularly invited her for coffee and Kugelhupf (a pastry). This endearing lady was personal assistant to a millionaire lady living nearby, who later invited my mother and me for occasional teas. One day the millionaire lady died and left a fortune. She had set aside enough for her faithful assistant of more than thirty-five years to buy a home and retire comfortably. Our friend said that she had more than she needed. So my mother suggested that she invest some of the extra money in an estate we had hoped to buy. She agreed and my mother's dream of living in an elegant estate came true. My mother's father had grown up in an estate. He was a descendant of Austria-Hungarian nobility. Two World Wars and personal tragedy had wiped away all the inheritance and savings of my grandparents and parents, leaving them penniless—as had happened to so many during both wars. But by way of this dear Polish lady, God answered a prayer and fulfilled my mother's heart's desire in her later years. According to rumors, this home was originally built as a summer "cottage" for the Vanderbilt grandchildren. Surrounded by one and a half acres of park-like greens, a wild rose garden and magnificent trees, this house was called Shady Lawn. It harbored ten fireplaces throughout three floors, a tower with views to the ocean and a separate coach house. The servants' quarters, used in earlier days, had a separate entrance and stairway.

17

We certainly couldn't afford any servants, so we had plenty of room to renovate and use most of this estate as a guesthouse and motel. My mother thrived in this environment. She was the perfect hostess, welcoming everyone with a heart of gold. Occasionally, famous people like Joan Baez or "Mr. Schweppes" visited this gracious place we called home.

God had brought our family from under the rubble of World War II to this fairy tale environment of gilded mansions, ocean breezes and pleasures of fine art. However, God led me later to a path that was devoid of such extravagance but that bestowed eternal values more precious than gold.

CHAPTER 4

MORE PRECIOUS
THAN GOLD

Upon my college graduation, I was employed as a foreign language teacher in a Christian liberal arts college in Barrington, Rhode Island. I seemed to spend more time counseling students than correcting their homework and tests. Soon I realized that I was more concerned about people's hearts than about their education, although I had ability to tend to both.

After two years of teaching there, I had the great privilege of hearing about Francis Schaeffer, who later became a well-known Christian author and philosopher. I decided to embark on another journey into the unknown. I resigned from teaching to study under this man's inspiration. His brilliant intellect, coupled with great compassion and Christian faith sparked a new fire in my heart. He and his family lived high up in the Swiss Alps, overlooking magnificent glistening glaciers and deep, lush, green valleys. Some farmers would take their cows up the mountains to graze, and their cowbells resounded like an orchestra in joyful celebration.

It was there at L'Abri, as the Schaeffer's home was called, that I asked God to anoint my piano playing with His music and song. It was there that I began to compose sacred music in glory to His name. It was there that I met the love of my life, a missionary's son who later was killed in a car crash. It was there that God surrounded me with His presence again and renewed my love for Him and my desire to serve Him.

One winter's night, upon receiving some disturbing news, I ran up the hills through woods and fields to find a place to cry and pray. I found a shack filled with hay and, with my face buried in my hands, I cried to the Lord. Soon I was comforted and immersed in an inexplainable peace. I simply basked in this wonderful, calming balm without realizing night had fallen. I covered myself with hay in the hopes of surviving the night there, but the air became unbearably cold. Finally, I headed out into the darkness. Shivering, I went faster and faster through the thick black forest. When I arrived at the edge of the woods and saw the village lights, I wondered how on earth I managed to come down this dark mountain so quickly without fear or falling. I turned around to view the path of my descent. To my astonishment, I saw the path behind me all lit up and lined with hovering angels.

By then it was two or three A.M. When I saw a light still burning in the Schaeffer's guest study, I knocked, and my beloved opened the door saying, "My dear, your face is lit up like an angel." I simply nodded and told no one what had occurred.

After these mountaintop experiences, the Lord led me to return to the United States in the spring of 1967. That summer I worked in an orphanage in New York State. After two hours of working there, I had mumbled to the Lord, "I don't want to work here!" He simply replied, "You are not working here, I AM!" This statement challenged me to stay and to find out exactly what God meant. I ended up working there for four and a half years. I was totally enthralled by the need, hunger and responsive hearts of these children and by how God was touching their lives.

It was a sacrifice to make. The hours were long, the pay was practically nothing, housing was modest and recognition was nil. Here on earth it was a silent, hidden task; but in the heavens, there was rejoicing, as child after child received the

Savior's love into their hearts. The hardest part wasn't managing a household of ten to fourteen children, but minding every broken little heart, soothing wounds, diminishing despair, binding hostility and loosening love. I soon realized that these tender souls were like pearls that could only be found in deep, deep waters. One could go there only by leaving a secure way of life behind. But in the end, the children proved to be more precious than gold and more valuable than any jewel on earth, having been bought by the Blood of the Lamb.

One crucial moment occurred not long after a six-year-old girl arrived. She was in a daze and unable to connect to her new environment. One day she briskly stomped out the front door, down the steps and across acres of fields firmly announcing, "I'm running away!" It all happened so quickly. "Take charge," I shouted to the oldest child, who was thirteen. I instinctively ran after the forlorn runaway. I finally caught up with her, took her in my arms and whispered, "I love you, sweetie, and Jesus loves you." As if awakening from a nightmare she replied, "Who? Who? Really?" I repeated my statement and asked her if I could tell her more about Jesus in the warmth of the house. She cautiously agreed and, as if relieved, let me take her hand to walk with her back to the house. Back inside, I wrapped her in a blanket, gave her some hot chocolate and softly told her how much God loved her and wanted to take care of her. Two days later, she accepted Jesus into her heart and overflowed with more joy than I had ever seen in a child. She told everyone of her newly found joy in Jesus and became the most loving and giving child in the orphanage.

A few weeks later, one of the children was hit in the face by a baseball and got knocked over. Her face was as white as a ghost. The children and I hovered over her while the six-year-old who had accepted the Lord reached over to the injured child and prayed a most fervent prayer. Within minutes, the pale-faced child regained color and strength and started laughing and bubbling with joy. Soon we were all laughing with delight and some children danced, shouting, "It's a miracle; it's a miracle!" For me these were precious, unforgettable moments to remember on days that seemed tedious and futile. These were moments that left an indelible mark on my heart, because I knew that God was moving in our midst.

On another day, after my mother had died, I was grievously depressed. Soon it affected all the children, and I cried to the Lord to lift our spirits and to come to my aid. Within the hour I suddenly heard the most heavenly music, like angels' choirs, that soothed my heart like a lullaby. This continued all night and into the next day. I seemed to be the only one hearing the music, so I asked God to also comfort and cheer up the little children around me and to fill them with His Holy Spirit. Suddenly one girl started laughing and laughing. It was so cheerful and contagious that, pretty soon, we were all laughing with continuous, joyous laughter. When we would stop, someone else would start again. This went on for hours, until bedtime. The next morning, one seven-year-old girl woke up singing in a new, heavenly language. She kept saying, "I'm so happy! I don't know what I'm singing, but I'm so happy!" I prayed for interpretation of her song, and soon she came to me, pointing her little finger upward. She explained, "I know what I'm singing. It means 'Thank you God.'" Her gesture was like a picture worth a million words. Her cheerfulness reverberated in everyone's heart, and, once again, we were thankful for God's joy and presence among us.

This children's home, out in the country, was like a ship in the middle of the sea that carried us onward in the voyage of our lives, through all kinds of days: playful and working days, sunny and stormy days. Some of the children had already experienced brutally violent storms. One child had witnessed her father murdering her pregnant mother, then raping and impregnating her older sister. Another had jumped out of a second-story window. Still another had ripped her arm open by pushing it through a glass door in defiance of household rules. Two young children had been found abandoned in a freezing New York City apartment. All the adversities of life had played out in these young children's hearts. By the time they came to live in this house on a hill overlooking serene fields, they had already experienced a kaleidoscope of human drama. They had seen love and hatred; bonding and abandonment; life and death; pleasure and pain; hope and despair; loyalty and betrayal, and comfort and cruelty. Now, in a safer environment, they embarked on a difficult journey of coping with the past while courageously moving on towards an uncertain future.

How I prayed for God to keep these young hearts safely anchored in *Him* on their voyage through life. These children, who are like jewels in His hand, are more precious to Him than gold.

Chapter 5

When God Speaks

A FEW MONTHS after my mother's death in 1969, my beloved fiancé, the missionary's son I had met in Switzerland, decided to experiment with drugs. He overdosed and was committed to a mental clinic for several months. He had given me a choice to join his indulging in drugs—something he had previously vowed never to experiment with—or else break off our relationship. Hurt and stunned I asked, "You mean, you're expecting me to choose between drugs and Jesus—between you and God?" He simply replied, "Yes." When I reminded him of my commitment to serve God, he left. I never saw him again.

It was as if the bottom fell out from under my feet. I proceeded to fall into a pit of endless despair. The two most important people in my life, my mother and my fiancé, were gone. Furthermore, my father had temporarily disowned me for dating a devout Catholic during my college years. At that time he believed the dating to be religious treason but later regretted it. Little did he know that at that time this fine gentleman had been instrumental in restoring my faith in God and in the saving knowledge of Jesus Christ, ending a short but profound period of spiritual perplexity in my life.

My biggest question in those days had been why God allowed suffering in the world. It is an age-old question that has puzzled theologians and people in general for many hundreds of years. Eventually, I found my answers in the Scriptures and in the presence of God revealed by the power of the Holy Spirit in everyday life. I discovered that the answer to this profound question is rooted in the grace, holiness and justice of God. It is also in man's crucial choice whether or not to acknowledge God's holiness and to receive His grace.

> And they sing the song of Moses, the servant of God, and the song of the Lamb, saying, "Great and marvelous are Your works, Lord God Almighty! Just and true are Your ways, O King of the saints!"
>
> —REVELATION 15:3

> Exalt the Lord our God,
> And worship at His footstool—
> He is holy . . . Exalt the Lord our God,
> and worship at His holy hill;
> For the Lord our God is holy.
>
> —PSALM 99:5,9

Since the Bible describes God as just and holy, I realized that His love and grace are based on His holiness. If He did not allow the world to experience suffering and death as a consequence of sin, we would never know the extent of the abomination and destructive power of sin. Likewise, we would not know the immeasurable height and depth of God's love and grace, revealed to us in His Son Jesus Christ.

Since the beginning of time God has continually spoken and reached out His hand to deliver us from evil and its destructive forces. Throughout the ages God has communicated His desire to restore our relationship with Him. In the beginning, God spoke creation into existence. Since then, He has spoken by way of His handiwork.

> The heavens declare the glory of God;
> And the firmament shows His handiwork.
>
> —PSALM 19:1

God has also spoken through His prophets, through His Son's presence on earth, through miracles and through the written Word. He is communicating to us that *He* is there, that *He* is holy, and that *He* wants to deliver us by restoring our relationship with *Him*. Moreover, God speaks to us through His Holy Spirit. Before Jesus departed from this earth, He declared:

> And I will pray the Father, and He will give you another Helper, that He may abide with you forever.
>
> —JOHN 14:16

> But when the Helper comes, whom I shall send to you from the Father, the Spirit of Truth who proceeds from the Father, He will testify of Me.
>
> —JOHN 15:26

> But you shall receive power when the Holy Spirit has come upon you.
>
> —ACTS 1:8

God continues to speak through His Holy Spirit, His written Word and His miracle working power. When God speaks are we listening? Are we heeding His Word which is a torch that lights the way through the darkest night, an anchor in the wildest storms, a rock in the sinking sand, a stream in the desert and an open door in the prisons of the soul?

> Your word is a lamp to my feet
> And a light to my path.
>
> —PSALM 119:105

This hope we have as an anchor of the soul, both sure and steadfast, and which enters the Presence behind the veil.

—HEBREWS 6:19

From the brightness before Him,
His thick clouds passed with hailstones and coals of fire.

—PSALM 18:12

One way we know that a person is present and alive is when we hear that person speak. And one of the ways we know that God is there and that Jesus is alive is to hear His voice.

My sheep hear My voice, and I know them, and they follow Me.

—JOHN 10:27

I was truly challenged to learn how to discern God's voice and how to listen when God speaks. I met a lady dying of cancer. According to the doctors, she had two months to live. One night, as she was contemplating suicide, she heard God audibly calling her by name. She was startled, but then she asked God if He was really there to send someone to her aid. The following night a Christian couple who lived next door knocked at her door. They said God had awakened them from their sleep and urged them to pray for her in person. She agreed, not telling them of her serious plight. While they prayed, she felt a warm sensation all over her body. A few days later her doctor discovered that her cancer had totally disappeared.

A few weeks after meeting this lady, I met a pastor who was prompted by the Lord to call a church office one Saturday evening and to share his overflowing joy. The pastor of that particular church had been praying and studying in the office when a man came in, pointing a gun at him and saying, "I just killed someone and you're next." Just then the phone rang. The intruder told the pastor to answer it. Through the telephone, the man with the gun heard loud, joyful praises to God, repeated many times. As he listened, he started to tremble, dropped the gun and ran out the door.

These incidents made a profound impression on my heart as I realized that God cared enough to intervene. In these cases he intervened by speaking directly or by way of another person who heeded His Word and instruction. "When God speaks, am I listening?" That became a question I have asked myself daily in the ensuing years.

The time following my mother's death and my fiancé's desertion was one of grief, loneliness and despair. I wanted to lie down and die. But I happened to come across a special anointed man of God. When he prayed for me, heaven seemed to open up and fill my heart with God's comfort, love and glory. I relished the awesome beauty and exquisite peace and holiness surrounding and filling me. After basking in this state for several days, God asked me, as He had done before, if I was willing to lay down my life for *Him*. After serious and sober consideration, I finally said *yes.* Soon after that, God called me to share the full gospel and to make disciples of people who were willing to pick up their crosses to follow Him. I was continuing my journey in life, clinging to God's love and power and to every single word He would whisper to me and confirm through Scripture, circumstances or the counsel of other believers. More and more I realized that heeding God's voice was essential to restoring and developing an intimate relationship with Him. My ability to hear His voice was in direct proportion to my willingness to follow Him at all costs.

> Then He said to them all, "If anyone desires to come after Me, let him deny himself, and take up his cross daily, and follow Me" . . . Then it happened, as they were parting from Him, that Peter said to Jesus, "Master, it is good for us to be here."
>
> —LUKE 9:23, 33

One of the first practical instructions the Lord revealed to me was to buy a car that was red with white on top. I thought that quite peculiar at first, since I had no money and no idea where to find such a car. One day, He told me to go to the post office. I resisted this instruction, arguing that I needed nothing there. But then I thought I should heed God's leading. On the way to the post office, I stopped at a traffic light behind a car that was red with white on top. I jumped out of my car, walked to the car in front of me and politely asked the lady driver if she knew where I could buy a car like this.

She thought for a minute, then said, "No, I don't, but I don't see why I couldn't sell you this one. Would you like to follow me home, so we can discuss this and make proper arrangements?" I did. Upon double checking with her husband, she quoted me a very fair price.

"Could I pay you in installments?" I stuttered.

"Sure," she said, "as long as it's within the next few weeks."

"That'll be fine," I agreed, having no idea how God was going to provide.

Within two weeks, I gave her my whole paycheck as first payment. Then God lead me to apply for a loan in a nearby bank. When they declined my request I muttered, "But Lord, you told me to come here."

The loan officer said, "I beg your pardon?"

I answered, "Oh, never mind. I thought for sure I'd get a loan here."

Two days later, I called him and asked, "Are you sure I can't get a loan?"

He replied, "Oh, I'm sorry; we made a mistake. We can lend you $1,000, but no more."

"I'll take it! I'll take it!" I exclaimed, trying to sound composed. I rushed to the bank and then to the lady's house. She was delighted but informed me that she needed the rest of the payments sooner than expected due to a change of plans. Two weeks later I again gave her my pay check, but I needed another $500. Frantically, I prayed and prayed. Within that week I was informed by the director of the orphanage that all employees who had worked there at least three years (I had been there for four) were about to receive a government check for back pay because we hadn't been paid for overtime. The check, to my amazement, amounted to the rest of my car payment with a few dollars left over. I was astonished that God would care about such mundane issues in my life.

From then on, I realized that nothing was unimportant or insignificant to Him. I ventured out to keenly discern His directions in my life, no matter how perplexing or trivial they seemed initially.

Within a few months, I resigned from the orphanage and followed God's leading to travel west across the United States. While on the road, my obedience and willingness to listen were tested again and again. God specifically warned me one afternoon to slow down while traveling on a freeway. Again I argued but then resigned myself to heeding His warning. Within two minutes a terrible five-car accident occurred in front of me. Had I not slowed down when I did, I would have crashed right into it, unable to stop in time. I trembled, both in the loving fear of the Lord and in thinking what might have happened had I not listened and obeyed. Timing was the big issue—possibly an issue of life and death.

A few days later, God impressed on me to exit the freeway and go to a specific farm. The cows on the farm seemed curious about what I was doing there. So was I! I prayed, candidly expressing my thoughts, "This is nice, but what am I doing here, Lord?" There was no answer. Suddenly, I noticed a dog nursing twelve puppies. I remembered a friend of mine, a few weeks earlier, had prayed for a pet to be my traveling companion. I had said to her, "Oh, no. I don't want a pet!" But God knew better. One of the puppies got up and bravely trotted to where I was sitting. It

30

climbed into the sleeve of my dress and curled up. It was love at first sight. I requested permission from the farmer to let me keep the puppy. He agreed happily. This little puppy became my best friend, companion and protector on many travels ahead.

Soon it became clear to me that this dog was not only my companion but also a witness for the Lord. One day, he was running around in circles, hissing and foaming from his mouth. I prayed in Jesus' name for healing and then cast out the demons plaguing him, demanding that they never return. He was instantly and permanently cured. But several weeks later, he was run over by a car and paralyzed in both hind legs. I cried and cried, until the Lord gently said, "I'll heal him in the morning." Morning came, and my puppy wasn't healed.

"But you promised, Lord!" I sobbed.

He replied, "But the morning isn't over yet."

True, true, I thought and went about my business. At 11:30 A.M. I looked out the kitchen window and there was my puppy, limping on three legs. I was ecstatic and cried for joy, hugging my puppy. The next day I took him to a vet to check the unused leg. It was broken. The vet put on a cast which was to stay on for at least six weeks. Ten days later the cast came off. I rushed him to the vet who took an X-ray. "It's a miracle; he's healed!" he exclaimed. That was some remark coming from an atheist!

I asked the Lord why Satan would attack and torment a little puppy.

He answered me, "Because I will use your puppy as a witness to the children." A few months later, I arrived on California's southwest coast in a town near the Pacific Ocean. My adorable puppy started to run away from home. The first time this happened I was very upset. God reassured me and said, "Wherever the children are, there is your dog." From then on, as I looked and listened for children in the neighborhood, I would always find my puppy playing in the midst of a small gathering of children. I would then tell them how God had healed my puppy, and we would talk about Jesus' love, sometimes singing familiar Sunday School songs together. The Lord truly used my little missionary dog for His glory.

The Lord confirmed to me again and again that listening to Him when He speaks can be a matter of life and death. One such occurrence was during a snowstorm in New York State in 1975, while I was visiting my sister. I was strongly urged by the Lord to visit a handicapped friend in Massachusetts. Having left my car in California, I tried to persuade my brother-in-law to give me a ride to the bus, but he refused. I stomped one mile through deep snow to catch the last bus. When I arrived the next morning at my friend's house, she didn't answer the door. In freezing weather, I waited and knocked, and waited and knocked again. Finally, I asked neighbors where she was. Nobody knew. I called all the churches in the neighborhood and finally found a pastor who knew her well. He and his wife allowed me to spend the night at their house.

The next day, they accompanied me to my friend's house. We knocked repeatedly at her door, but to no avail. When she heard our combined voices calling her name, she answered the door. After two hours of helping her and listening to her, she confided in me that for two days she had locked herself in, contemplating suicide. Her circumstances were difficult enough to throw her into a state of despondency. Within a few hours of consoling and praying with her, though, her whole outlook on life and on her particular problems changed from despair to determination to seek God for an answer. It ended up being not only a lifesaving occasion for her, but a wonderful reunion for both of us and her young child.

Another dramatic incident occurred one summer evening in Denver, Colorado. God alerted me of an imminent murder. Stunned, I prayed all night for God's intervention. The next evening I happened to take part in street witnessing with a group of young people. One girl and I encountered a drunken man. Upon our sweet, innocent invocation, "God loves you," he showed us a knife and said, "See this knife? I'm going to kill a guy in that bar tonight."

We were aghast and speechless for a second, not knowing whether to run, to pray or to call the police. For some reason, we said to him, "Would you like for us to pray for you first?"

Somehow that didn't sound right, but to our relief and great astonishment he replied, "Why not? I got nothing to lose." While we prayed, he started to weep uncontrollably. He got on his knees right in the gutter and repented, asking God to help him change. In the meantime, the group had caught up with us, and we rejoiced in God's protection and convicting power.

One summer day in California, I opened the Yellow Pages, looking for work. God impressed on me to call one particular phone number. Again I argued, "Oh, no Lord. I don't want to work there!" But I finally obeyed and called.

A rich, cheerful masculine voice answered. "Praise the Lord!"

"Well, praise the Lord indeed," I enthusiastically replied. "Do you need any child care workers?' I asked, hoping he would say no.

"Praise the Lord," he remarked again. "Come right over. Can you start tomorrow? We've been praying for a Christian worker for six weeks!"

How could I refuse? So I went for the interview and started the next day. It was a Christian home for handicapped and severely retarded children. The children's mental capacity was between one and three years of age, even though some were sixteen-years-old. It was heart breaking to see them at first, but within a couple of hours I realized what a beautiful, innocent and kind spirit these children exhibited. In the end, they were a profound blessing to me. I continued for about two years to care for them, pray for them and sing to them.

Once during the night shift, after I had prayed for each child,

I heard someone singing. I checked on the oldest child who was the only one able to say a few words; but he was sleeping. I followed the singing and found a blind, nine-year-old boy who had never said a word in his life. He was singing "Hallelujah, hallelujah." Another day, God urged me to drop my work and dash into the next room. There I found a girl in an epileptic fit. I quietly laid my hands on her head and prayed. Instantly her shaking stopped, and she smiled the most beautiful smile. These were divine moments in the lives of these children who are to God more precious than silver or gold.

As time went on, I realized the difference one person can make in someone's life. Indeed, one person can even change the course of history for many people—for better or for worse. When the captain of the *Titanic* refused to heed repeated warnings about icebergs, he chose the course of disaster and death for hundreds of people. Fortunately, many individuals throughout history heeded God's Word and were instrumental in the deliverance and prosperity of peoples and nations. God's Son heeded the Father's voice and paid the ultimate price to save us.

What price are we willing to pay to heed God's Word and to be an instrument of His love and rescuing mercies? When God speaks, am I listening? This is the question I continually face throughout the journey of my life. It is a question that challenges me to seek God's presence daily and to embark on the voyage He has ordained by His grace.

CHAPTER 6

HAND IN HAND

A S THE SUNNY or rainy, calm or turbulent days on the voyage of my life continued, I became intrigued by observing the networks of people God knits together to fulfill His purposes. These networks serve not only as expressions of His love and loyalty but also as instruments of restoration and deliverance. They are safety nets for those falling and sinking into sin or despair. The networks also serve as mighty armies and spectacular fleets overcoming enemy forces and violent storms while advancing triumphantly to conquer their rightful shores.

I have had the opportunity of working as a teacher and counselor in various schools and institutions. I have also worked as a governess and tutor in many different homes. This enabled me to observe many kinds of family dynamics. I experienced the power of family unity as it produces intimacy and bonding; loyalty and responsibility; joy and compassion, and creativity and growth in each member. A close knit family is like a well functioning organism, pulsating with invigorating rhythms of love. As family members walk hand in hand, they form a strong bond and an intimate network of kin. They exude stability, confidence and strength. These God given attributes seem to improve as they permeate to the extended family, the entire family tree, the church family and to the community. Like ripples that spread across the waters when touched by one hand, the power of God's love flows freely from the cubicles of a caring family life to wider and wider circles of humanity.

Unfortunately, I have also observed and experienced firsthand the devastating and crippling effects that disharmony and disconnectedness can bring. Some families live together, but inwardly they are at war, ripping one another apart and severing the tie that carries the sustenance of love and life.

> But He, knowing their thoughts, said to them, "Every kingdom divided against itself is brought to desolation, and a house divided against a house falls."
>
> —LUKE 11:17

By God's grace these ties can be restored and mended through much prayer, forgiveness and wise counsel. By God's healing power and fire of love, we can walk again, hand in hand, lifting one another up when one falls, crying with those who cry and dancing with those who dance. It is by receiving God's love and by our love for one another that the Body of Christ, the Temple of the Holy Spirit, is repaired and prepared to receive God's blessing, glory and deliverance.

> This is My commandment, that you love one another as I have loved you.
>
> —JOHN 15:12

> My little children, let us not love in word or in tongue, but in deed and in truth.
>
> —1 JOHN 3:18

> Those from among you Shall build the old waste places; You shall raise up the foundations of many generations; And you shall be called the Repairer of the Breach, The Restorer of Streets to Dwell In.
>
> —ISAIAH 58:12

In reaching out in love and walking hand in hand, we bless one another as His Word commands. We must bless by loving one another—not only in word but also in thought and deed. Furthermore, it is important to bless those who curse us, in order to provide a tool for restoration.

> They bless with their mouth,
> But they curse inwardly.
> —PSALM 62:4

> Bless those who persecute you; bless and do not curse.
> —ROMANS 12:14

> Bless those who curse you, and pray for those who spitefully use you.
> —LUKE 6:28

> But I say to you, love your enemies, bless those who curse you, do good to those who hate you, and pray for those who spitefully use you and persecute you.
> —MATTHEW 5:44

We bless with our words and thoughts as well as with our deeds. One gentle smile can bless someone who, in turn, gains the strength to bless others. One kind word or deed can restore a wilting soul to life. What price are we willing to pay in order to bless someone on this earth? God sent His only begotten Son to die for us on Calvary that we might live and that all mankind may be blessed with grace and fellowship with *Him.* Jesus paid the ultimate price to bless us. Many missionaries have paid a tremendous price to bring the gospel to people around the world. Great men in history have risked their lives to bless their lands and their kings and queens. There have been scores of heroes, since the beginning of time, who were willing to give all to bless where cursing had crippled human lives. American history alone abounds with heroic pioneers like Christopher Columbus, George Washington, Abraham

Lincoln, and Dwight Eisenhower. God inspired these people, and they risked all in order to bless millions of people with hope, abundance and freedom. They blessed by being willing to give their lives. But Jesus made the ultimate sacrifice and became the living link between God and man. On the cross He bore the curses of sin and death to bless all mankind with eternal life. He blessed us by heeding the Father's wish as He proclaimed, "Not my will, but *thine* be done." When God speaks, are we listening? When He beckons, are we reaching out a hand of blessing to revive a weak and wilting soul?

Many of us have had heroes in our lives—people who made a difference at a crucial point in time. I have always found it much more pleasant to be a hero in someone's life, than to need one myself. However, I found that needing one at times ensures my humility and ability to better empathize with others in distress.

One of the first heroes in my life was my mother, who nurtured me to health during a severe case of diphtheria at age four or five. The children's wing in the hospital was still in shambles from the bombing, and my mother refused to send me to the adult section of the hospital, fearing I would not survive. Penicillin was not yet available. According to the doctor, it was unlikely that I would survive the illness, but my mother held me day and night, praying for me, loving me and applying cold wet wraps to bring the fever down. She blessed me with her tender loving care. She kept her praying arms around me and her song beside me.

Some of my latest heroes on the sometimes stormy voyage of my life are a pastor and two friends. Within a period of eighteen months I had been struggling with several losses of loved ones and acquaintances. While I, myself, was being treated for a previously misdiagnosed and potentially fatal illness, my dad and then my best friend died of cancer. Then, in intervals of several weeks each, ten acquaintances unexpectedly passed away. It felt like I was living in the "twilight zone." My grieving was intense. I had barely begun to cope with these painful losses when I learned that my ex-fiancé, the love of my life who had been searching for me, was tragically killed in a car crash.

Many friends abandoned me because of my continual deep sorrow due to the loss of several loved ones. Soon no one in the church cared to sympathize and help relieve my agony and pain. Even my oldest sister, whose Christian testimony in previous years had been like a torch in a dark sky, ignored my desolation. To add insult to injury, her unfounded slander (for which she later apologized) prompted some of her family members to sever their relationships with me.

During this traumatic time, I was drowning in grief and immersed in agony. Bitterness pervaded my heart like arsenic in a glass of wine. I was plagued with a sense of doom, and I feared being overcome with grief and fainting at the wheel while driving.

One Sunday morning in church, the pastor announced at the end of the sermon, "I have a deep burden to pray for someone in fear of dying prematurely." My heart was touched indeed for God to care enough to intervene and for this pastor to have compassion to be willing to heed God's prompting. As he prayed for me, the Holy Spirit poured like oil into the wounds of sorrow and hurt, softly breaking apart my sense of panic and despair. God's anointing through one man's outstretched hand relieved my agony and pain enough for me to go on living and healing.

In the ensuing months, my grieving heart was still quite weak, and I prayed for God to send a friend who would walk with me and help me mend. This prayer was soon answered when Lorraine Gutowsky, a colleague on a weekend job, crossed my path to quiet my intense distress. For hours she would listen to my pitiful stories over hot tea and homemade cookies, until there was no more to tell. She put her heart and arms around me and walked the second mile with me. From day to day, she cared and prayed and lent a listening ear. Through her unceasing, loving care and company, the grief torn sails in my weary soul slowly mended to catch the wind of God's Holy Word that provides us with direction and with power to cross the deep waters of our lives.

A short time later, God sent another friend along my path. Mary Collett, a retired nurse, appeared like a good Samaritan at a time when I was sick with the flu. I was destitute and without a job or a place to live. When Mary heard about my plight, she offered me a place in her home and in her heart. She invited me to spend Christmas with her and her son's family. This was a welcomed miracle for me, since I could no longer bear the cruel experience of spending Christmas alone while grieving and watching everyone else feasting in their families' love and company. Her open heart provided me with hope and a steady grip while I was climbing the treacherous mountain of broken dreams. On foggy, rainy days, when I could see no rhyme or reason in my life, she would cheer me on and reach out a generous hand.

In order to be an instrument of restoration, love and unity, it is most important, when we're hurting, to provide the opportunity for ourselves to heal and to be restored. In taking on the responsibility of seeking our own restoration, growth and healing, we bless ourselves and in turn are able to be a blessing and an instrument of unity, restoration and growth for others. There are many ways by which we can ensure blessings upon our own lives and also become a blessing. In order to receive God's blessing it is essential to heed His Word.

> ... blessed are those who keep my ways.
> Blessed is the man who listens to me ...
> But he who sins against me wrongs his own soul.
> —PROVERBS 8:32, 34, 36

So that he who blesses himself in the earth shall bless
himself in the God of truth.

—Isaiah 65:16

Blessed is the man who fears the Lord,
Who delights greatly in His commandments.

—Psalm 112:1

Blessed are those who do His commandments.

—Revelation 22:14

Blessed are the merciful . . . Blessed are the pure in heart.

—Matthew 5:7, 8

He who has clean hands and a pure heart,
Who has not lifted up his soul to an idol . . .
He shall receive blessing from the Lord.

—Psalm 24:4-5

Blessed is the man who trusts in the Lord, and whose
hope is the Lord.

—Jeremiah 17:7

Blessed is the man whose strength is in You.

—Psalm 84:5

Blessed are all those who wait for Him.

—Isaiah 30:18

When we are too weak to ensure blessings for ourselves, or
when our own families fail to bless us and, thus, refuse to
allow God's healing restoration to flow through them, our
Heavenly Father will provide us with His care.

When my father and my mother forsake me,
Then the Lord will take care of me.

—Psalm 27:10

Moreover, the Body of Christ needs to be available to provide a rescuing hand in times of such distress. In so doing, we, as the family of God, are blessing those who are being cursed and those who are cursing us. We become the extension of God's hand that continually seeks to draw mankind into His presence to attain a personal relationship with Him. Are we willing to be instruments of God's blessing hand and break the curses in our lives and in the lives of those around us? Are we listening to know when we are to lend a hand to help someone carry his load and ease his pain? Are we prepared to offer an out-stretched arm to guide someone to God's presence where there is healing, deliverance and joy? When we walk hand-in-hand in His Kingdom of blessing and compassion, His healing and restoration flow and His love and power are made manifest in us, our families, our churches and our communities.

CHAPTER 7

ROYAL OFFSPRING

FOR MORE THAN a decade before the following episode in my voyage through life, God had clearly spoken to me with these words, "I will open your mouth before princes." At first, I thought He surely must be addressing the wrong person. After considerable attempts to find an explanation, I dismissed the whole matter. I put it in the back of my mind like a misunderstood book on a hidden bookshelf gathering cobwebs and dust.

However, during some of the sunnier, funnier days of my life's journey, God's Word once again proved to be true.

In the spring of 1989 God gave me the opportunity to get another glimpse of the ways of the wealthy. I was traveling through sun scorched plains, abandoned highways and gentle hills bearing the promises of spring to a new job as a governess in Greenwich, Connecticut. My little Toyota hatchback was stuffed with boxes and plants. Somehow I managed to find space on the ledge of the back window for my cat who leisurely watched the countryside unfold all the way from the Colorado Rockies to the Rhode Island shores. There I stopped to greet old friends. I also walked along the rose-hemmed cliffs and paid homage to Shady Lawn, our elegant family estate of yesteryear. I stood there like a visitor at someone's grave site, as I gazed at the home where I once had enjoyed the company of my parents. I struggled with facing the grim reality that they were gone from this earth. Fortunately, the memories of laughter, music and romance that this house evoked drowned out the painful groaning of grief that grew within my heart. How much I wished I could turn back the clock to ring the doorbell and embrace the warmth of family love. It took courage to walk on, but the pleasant memories accompanied me and gave me comfort and reassurance.

Within a day or two, I began my new employment. It was an exotic job; I was governess to a young boy, in the home of an accountant to one of the wealthiest American television comedians. The house was being remodeled, so I was lodged in a nearby exquisite Victorian bed and breakfast hotel surrounded by lush green gardens that were laced with fragrant dogwood trees and brightly blooming Forsythia bushes. It could have been straight out of a picture book.

During working hours, I cared for the boy in his home where there were a butler, a chef, a housekeeper, an ironing lady and a gardener. We were served gourmet food for lunch and dinner.

One day I was instructed to take the boy to the zoo, so I politely requested a map and directions. I was told, "Oh, you won't need a map; the limousine will take you." To this I had no objection at all! The next morning, a limousine waited for us while the boy had breakfast. Then it transported us to the nearest airport. In protest I exclaimed, "Oh, there must be a mistake, sir. We're supposed to go to the zoo!"

"Oh, I know," the chauffeur replied. "His favorite zoo is in Minneapolis. The plane is waiting over there." He pointed to a small private plane, which would whisk us off to Minneapolis. Once there, another limousine awaited us and drove us to the zoo, where a class of curious school children stared at us. One child asked, "Are you somebody famous?"

It caught me by surprise, so I stuttered, "No—not that I know of!"

The following week the boy, his mother, some of her friends, the butler and I flew in this same plane to Mystique, the most southern island of the West Indies. On board we were served lobster, caviar and champagne. The friendly blue skies and woolly ceiling of clouds seemed to embrace us with welcoming promises of grandiose pleasures of living. The waters below reflected the heavens like deep blue topaz, and the sunlight, like shimmering diamonds, danced on the surface of the water. Due to the slow ebbing of the tide, the hilly, emerald-green, lush islands seemed to rise from the sea.

We vacationed on the island of Mystique for two whole weeks in an ocean-front house that breathed in the sea breeze and exotic fragrances of blooming gardens. Palm trees swayed and danced the hula in the winds. The timeless tides continually called out and beckoned us to frolic in the invigorating currents of the crystal sea and to join them in their dance upon the white washed sand.

There were housekeepers, maids and a chef on duty every day. Again, we feasted on gourmet food. At night one of the maids drew a mosquito net around each bed and lit a hurricane lamp on the nightstand to deter bugs and tiny flying insects throughout the night. It was quite romantic and exotic.

One night, there was a house party to which some local villagers were invited. For entertainment there were dances to the typical native rag music. There were also fresh lobsters and crab, coconuts and caviar, champagne and wine. Some people had way too much to drink. Sometime past midnight, the butler and the mistress of the house vanished into the night. They reappeared the next afternoon, freely flaunting their affair for everyone to know. I excused myself to wander off in search of nearby virgin shores where young volcanic rocks were embedded in ancient sands that held the secrets of the past but left no imprint of the day before. Each tide had washed away every footprint made by man, leaving no trace of our existence—no mark for anyone to know that anyone had been there. In a way, it seemed like the surging sea of grace that washes us clean and leaves no trace of our sin. It invites us to start anew each morning and each forgiving day.

In the warm, shallow waters of these shores, I found enormous seashells resounding with deep, mysterious ocean tones. In the distance lay the remains of a trade ship that had crashed against a small island of volcanic rock. Like a memorial of days gone by, this defeated vessel remained unmoved. It seemed to be a warning for those traveling at sea to respect the power of the sea and to equip themselves in order to survive a ruthless storm.

"What was this vessel trading, anyway?" I asked. No one seemed to know for sure. One's imagination could go wild. Who was on board the ship? Did they drown, or did they make it to the shore? Were they trading food or fur, jewels or even slaves? The slave market had ended much earlier in the West Indies than in the United States, I learned later. The mulatto slaves of French and African origin united in fierce uprisings to overthrow their captors. They had succeeded and banished their oppression, having freed themselves with cunning, sweat and blood.

Somehow, the gospel of Jesus Christ had been passed down from original slave owners to their servants and to generations and generations of their kin. One Sunday morning, when I was off duty, I visited a local Christian church, where I heard the gospel preached with exhilarating fervor. Praises to God were sung in exquisite harmonies by the natives of the land who were distant offspring of the slaves. I politely asked them where the "white man" worshiped on this isle, and they remarked, "Oh, they don't come or have another church, but we pray for them. First, the white man gave us Jesus many years ago; now we pray to bring the gospel back to them."

Then I listened as they prayed and sang again with passion, their melodious voices traveling across the village and far out over the sea. This place of worship was, to me, like a rare pearl found in the depth of the sea—a pearl that would remind me again and again of God's pleasure and delight in a people that will pray and praise Him and walk in His statutes.

> For the Lord takes pleasure in His people;
> He will beautify the humble with salvation.
> —PSALM 149:4

> The sacrifice of the wicked is an abomination to the Lord,
> But the prayer of the upright is His delight.
> —PROVERBS 15:8

Before we returned to the United States and to another reality of life, we had the wonderful pleasure of sailing on a gigantic one hundred twenty foot schooner with four powerful masts and sails. It was rented for one day so that we could cross the shimmering, jewel-like waters and visit neighboring islands and towns. Upon our return, some of us, including myself, had enough adventurous spirit to jump thirty feet from the deck into the sea to swim awhile. Then we climbed up a rope ladder to join the more sensible travelers on board. It was an opportunity of a lifetime to "jump ship" from an ocean going vessel on a calm, sunny day. On our flight back, I wondered if life would ever be so good again. I wondered if it would ever be this gentle, soothing and kind.

About a year later, I was working as a governess in a home in Atlanta, Georgia. One night, the Lord distinctly impressed on my mind to pack my things. Somewhat startled, I thought to myself, *Oh, no! I can't afford to move again.* In reminiscing about past promptings of the Lord, I decided to follow God's leading no matter how peculiar it seemed. With a chuckle in my heart and curiosity in my mind, I secretly packed my belongings and waited for further guidance. I had no particular desire to go anywhere. Jokingly I said to myself, *Well, let's see, the only thing I haven't done yet is live in a castle.*

47

Two days later, I got a call from Betty, an agent for childcare positions, inquiring about my state of affairs. She brusquely asked me, "How would you like to live in a castle?"

I laughed and remarked, "Oh, that's funny! I was just jokingly thinking that the other day!"

"Oh, I'm not joking!" Betty exclaimed. "I'm serious; how would you like to live in a castle? Princess Alexandra from Germany called me yesterday. She is looking for a German-English speaking governess, and I told her there's only one person in the world who could fill that position—and that's you."

I could hardly believe my ears. Could this be true? The next day I had a telephone interview in German with Princess Alexandra. Apparently delighted with our conversation, she said, "My husband happens to be on a business trip in Atlanta tomorrow. Can you meet him?"

Can I meet him? I thought. I had never met a prince before. I agreed politely. The next day I appeared with all the graciousness I could muster before this refined, titled gentleman. He was as polite and kind as could be. Two days later I was officially hired. They asked me how soon I would come since they needed someone right away. I was walking on cloud nine. Fortunately, a teenage girl down the street from where I had been working had just started her summer vacation and was gladly available to fill my job. The timing was perfect for everyone involved.

Upon receiving a plane ticket in the mail and one month's salary in advance to take care of bills before I left this country, I bid farewell to family and friends and said hello to a new exciting future. I was traveling above the clouds as though on a ship with wings, and preparing myself for this new adventure in my life. I was praying for renewed energy in my feet and a clean spirit in my heart while clearly remembering and pondering the words God had spoken to me over a decade ago, "I will open your mouth before princes."

It was electrifying to see these words being fulfilled as the Lord filled my mouth with wisdom to share. Like an ambassador of the gospel of Jesus Christ, I had opportunities to share the wonderful news of God's forgiveness and resurrection power with many staff. I also shared God's Word with some of the relatives of the princess and with her four children, who were ages four, seven, nine and eleven. They were descendants of German kings and lived in two enormous medieval castles, both fully staffed with butlers, chefs, secretaries, housekeepers, laundry ladies and gardeners. These castles had been in the family for almost seven hundred fifty years. It was awesome to walk through their ancient halls lined with ironclad statues from the Middle Ages and portraits of more than twenty generations of ancestors. Both castles had been modernized with proper heating, running water and cheerful interior decorating amidst valuable antiques. Surrounding the castles were well manicured gardens, abounding with roses and majestic trees. The park-like gardens were graced with sculptured fountains. Steady bubbling sounds accompanied the songs of feathered friends as they flew in for a visit from nearby fields and forests. Every hour the tower bells proclaimed the time of day. On Sunday mornings, they welcomed inhabitants of the castles and of the nearby villages to join in holy mass and worship in one of the castles' gilded Baroque cathedrals. There was also a vegetable garden that supplied us with fresh vegetables and berries all summer long. A nearby farmhouse provided fresh eggs, bread and milk, while nearby fields provided grain for the castle and the adjacent village. There was separated housing for the butler, the chefs and the maids. The governess was the only member of the staff allowed to live in the castle, being the most privileged in the hierarchy of the staff and needing to be near the children—the royal offspring.

This aristocratic family was polite, warm, fun loving and cultured; yet down to earth and unpretentious. It was a joy and a privilege to serve and observe them. My job was to care for the children and teach them English. I also helped them with piano lessons, homework and recreation. To the parents' great delight, we gave a little summer concert on the lawns— playing instruments and singing together as a quintet. We also created a children's story that we transformed into a play. The children performed as I accompanied, improvising on the piano for musical background and effect. For the oldest girl, Francisca, I composed a short violin piece to encourage her newly found interest in violin.

One problem I encountered while working in this opulent environment was occasionally not being able to locate the children who went in four different directions and were nowhere to be found in these enormous royal dwellings. The walls were several feet thick and impenetrable by most human voices. My room was on the top floor of the castle near one of the rounded towers, so I couldn't hear where they were after bedtime. Another problem I encountered was my work schedule. I worked long hours, and my days off were unpredictable. As it turned out, I was on call from 6:30 A.M. to 11:00 P.M. every single day, except Sunday mornings when I went to church. As time went on I felt too isolated from society, friends and church activities. Most importantly, my best friend in the USA was struggling for her life, fighting breast cancer. Additionally my aging father was weakening due to pancreatic cancer. Although I didn't yet know that my dad and best friend would soon go to be with the Lord, I respectfully and amiably bid farewell with the blessing of the princess and her kin. After a quick trip to Austria, my home- land, and heartwarming visits with relatives and childhood friends, I returned to the USA.

Besides the enriching experiences acquired during this memorable time with the royal family of that country, I had gained new friendships on the way. One summer afternoon,

God urged me to take the children for ice cream at a nearby inn that graced the edge of the forest their parents owned. When we arrived, I heard beautiful Christian music, sung in German, coming from somewhere near the woods. I looked around and found a car from whence the music came. A lady was putting her baby in the car. I ran over to her and politely asked, "Guten Tag. May I ask you where you go to church? Are you perhaps a Christian?"

She turned and excitedly replied, "Why, yes!" Without hesitation, we embraced with overflowing joy, both of us having prayed for new Christian friends. It was the beginning of a long, enriching and caring friendship.

When God wants to guide us to hidden treasures in this life, are we listening? Are we listening when He wants us to share the riches of His joy? Are we listening when He wants us to share the provision and beauty of His majesty? When God speaks, are we listening?

Chapter 8

Shackles of Gold

ONE MORNING IN November 1995, during the time when I was embracing the generosity of my friend, Mary Collett, and residing in her Colorado home, the phone rang while I was in the shower. When I was finished, Mary shouted, "Oh, that was Betty on the phone."

I thought at first, *Betty who?* Then thinking aloud I exclaimed, "Not Betty Barnes! It couldn't be! I haven't seen her in years, how would she know I am here?" I called the number Betty left and she graciously answered in her New Zealand accent, "Hello, this is Betty ... "

I gasped and cheerfully replied, "Betty! What an incredible surprise—how ever on earth did you find me?"

A few days earlier God had impressed on my mind to call and give my new telephone number to an agent of child care positions who happened to be a friend of Betty. Since I felt this lady didn't like me too much, I had resisted calling her; but upon God's continual urging, I finally obeyed, gritted my teeth, and dialed her number. Fortunately a machine answered so I could simply leave my name and number. Two days later Betty had called her, asking if she had any idea where in the world I was these days. If I had not heeded God's prompting, Betty would not have known how to reach me.

Now she was able to contact me and inform me of the latest

news. "The Getty family is looking for a governess . . . are you available these days?"

Gulping with excitement, I tried to compose myself, then replied, "Am I available? Yes, indeed I am! Betty, are you talking about **the** Getty family?"

"The one in California—do you know them?" she inquired.

"Well, no," I exclaimed, "but they are only one of the richest families in the world!" She then asked me to send my resume, which she faxed to the Getty residence in California.

The next day I received a phone call from the butler, who was also head of the staff. "Your resume is quite impressive. Can you come for an interview?" he remarked with most gracious dignity and with the most exquisite English accent I had ever heard. When my answer was affirmative he added, "Oh, and we'll arrange for you to fly out, of course. Would next weekend work for you?" I was in ecstasy all week and wondered why God would snatch me from the valley of grieving the loss of several friends and relatives to such a high and lofty enterprise. The elasticity of the range of my emotions was being stretched to its very limits.

On the day of the interview, Mary was sharing my excitement and taking pictures of me all dressed up for this glamorous occasion. Then she took me to the airport, like a fairy godmother in a coach to Cinderella's ball. Her sweet words were soothing, inspiring a skip in my step and a joyful leap in my heart as I trotted off to catch the plane.

Once in San Francisco, I called the butler who apologized for the delay in the limousine's arrival. In his distinguished accent he requested, "Would you mind terribly to fetch a taxi? We will pay for it, of course." It was a little hard at first, to comprehend the gallantry of this apology, but I went along with this line of thinking and graciously accepted the "lesser" offer of taking a taxi rather than riding in a limousine.

As the balmy California air wafted through an open window,

the taxi made its way along the bay, through Chinatown and up the hills of San Francisco. The driver stopped in front of the requested address and curiously asked, "Are you visiting an embassy?" *What an appropriate remark,* I thought. It was reminding me that indeed I was an ambassador of Christ, embarking on another mission to serve and bless in Jesus' name.

The house did look somewhat like an embassy, with pillars in the front and fancy cars along the driveway. With the greatest anticipation, I rang the doorbell. The English butler opened the door and welcomed me with profound efficiency. I was led through an elegant hallway to the parlors of the house which were furnished with antiques, priceless museum pieces and works of art. In the adjacent enormous music room stood a gigantic Steinway grand piano that faced several dozen fancy chairs resting on an antique carpet.

As I looked out the tall, slender windows lined with silk and velvet curtains, my heart stopped for a second as I gazed at the ethereal view of Alcatraz. It glittered in sunset hues and seemed to rise above the early evening fog as if to free itself from its sordid history. Its radiant glow heralded, like a soul set free, its deliverance from a gloomy past. The mellow coastal breezes freely swept through open windows and down halls that once exuded the prisoners' stench of death and desperate profanities.

Beyond the sounds and silhouettes of seaborne ships appeared the Golden Gate Bridge, as if suspended in the air, gently brushed by mesmerizing evening mists that caressed the waters of the San Francisco Bay.

While I waited, a primly dressed maid served some tea, then disappeared in the labyrinth of doors. Actually, I started feeling quite at home, as the opulent environment fondly brought back exquisite memories of Newport days and enriching months in German medieval castles.

Finally, the butler returned, accompanied by the secretary,

who asked me a few questions. She also explained some of the job-related expectations. She also explained some of the traveling habits of this extraordinary, wealthy family. Then she added, "Mr. and Mrs. Getty are suffering today from backache and jet lag. Can you come back next week?"

"Of course," I gulped, "and thank you for flying me out here today." She briskly bid farewell and disappeared. The butler, as enchanting as could be, led me back to the front hall, graciously opening the tall, elegant door. He guided me down the steps and swung open the door of the limousine. "The car will take you to the airport. See you next week!" And off I went, smoothly riding over the hills of San Francisco and along the shimmering waters of the bay. The full moon, like an oversized silver plate, hovered in midair with hypnotizing, mysterious gleams.

The following week, I repeated this trip which cost around $1,200 dollars each time. I wondered if this extravagance would pay off for them. As I waited for the interview, I shyly, quietly glided across the ancient carpets in the music room. I sat down awhile to warm the piano bench and finally invoked enough nerve to softly tickle the ivory keys. Just then I heard a woman's voice, "Oh, you play the piano!" I was a little startled, but this unassuming lady then led me back to the fancy sitting room. She proceeded to explain the job description and offered me the opportunity to start as soon as possible. I finally realized I was talking to Mrs. Gordon Getty, who then introduced me to Mr. Getty and proceeded to ask me, "Do you have your passport with you? Can you fly with us to London in the morning? We'll be back the day before Thanksgiving." Well, I didn't, and I couldn't. I was not prepared for such a sudden, drastic change.

I spent Thanksgiving with my friends in Colorado, then returned to San Francisco to begin my new endeavor. I had barely arrived in the evening, when I was called on duty for the night shift, caring for a ten-month-old child. Looking out the stately windows upon a magnificent view of city lights and stars, the child and I watched with great delight the slowly moving lights of automobiles crossing the Golden Gate Bridge. The bridge looked like a string of lit up pearls around a sleeping giant's neck.

The next night, both the child and I were served gourmet food on silver trays, with silver spoons. This was a continual occurrence in the weeks to come. Maids cleaned every room in use each day; laundry ladies washed and ironed clothes. Florists arranged beautiful bouquets and decorated an extraordinary Christmas tree. A French chef and kitchen help prepared the meals, while designers helped remodel rooms. On my daily strolls with the young child, a security guard was usually to accompany us for safety reasons. Ten days before Christmas the child, the mother and her grandmother and I were taken by limousine to the Nutcracker ballet. Afterwards, the limousine drove the mother of the child and myself to a clothing store to outfit us with clothing for an upcoming ski trip.

On the very first weekend I was there, my friend Lorraine stopped to spend some time with me on her way to visit her relatives near San Francisco. How endearing it was to share with her the excitement as well as the apprehensions of my new job. On Christmas Eve, the house was empty; everyone had gone except the security guard. Mary arrived from Colorado to visit me, and we spent that Christmas with her son and family, about an hour from the San Francisco Bay. Her warm smiles and hugs enabled me to face a new year with new hope and strength.

The morning after Christmas day, the grandmother and I were driven by a limousine to the family plane. It was a good sized plane, luxuriously furnished inside. The child and the mother of the child, a group of friends, two pilots and a flight attendant were on board. We stopped in Newark, New Jersey and near London, England, to refuel, and finally arrived in Lyons, France.

A taxi awaited our arrival to take us to the world's largest ski lift area which provided 600 slopes and 200 ski lifts. We climbed the winding roads of snow-capped mountains until we reached the town of Mirabel, high in the French Alps. We resided in a five star hotel with breathtaking views of ice-cold mountains and their jagged peaks. The Alpine village harbored tourists from all over the world. From hidden memories of college years, my French was forced slowly into the surface of my mind.

On New Year's Eve, we watched some fireworks erupt like spitting fire onto the snow, defying the cold. One tiny Catholic church opened its doors to welcome strangers from all lands to celebrate our God and to invoke His Son, Jesus Christ our Savior, to be gracious unto us and bless the new beginnings of the year.

Inside the hotel there was music and some dancing. A French composer played his piano compositions and later complemented me on mine. It was an eventful evening indeed. After midnight, I couldn't sleep, so I built a fire in the fireplace and called my sister and my friends in the United States to wish them a Happy New Year—happy new beginnings. I also called my aunt in Munich and my friends in Austria. They were so surprised to hear that I might come to see them soon. After one and a half weeks of extravagant dining and daring cable car rides on steep and treacherous mountaintops, I took a few days off. I descended these glorious Alps by taxi and bus to catch a commercial plane in Geneva, Switzerland.

Unexpectedly, the plane flew over Lake Geneva and the mountain range that had witnessed and held embedded, like a treasured secret, my youth's sweet and innocent romance. Those were the hills that stretched forth their peaks, inviting my beloved and me to run through their verdant fields. We had proclaimed our love to one another in the presence of the mountain peaks that echoed in return. Now I sadly said good-bye to such sweet memories. *Will I ever love like that again?* I wondered, as the clouds engulfed the plane, gently blocking the view of this spot on earth where I once was loved.

Fortunately, my good friend Gitti, whom I had met hearing the music in her car when I was working in the castle near Augsburg, Germany, picked me up from the Munich airport. Her love and laughter helped me forget the past, for now. We relished our time together and the sweet fellowship we shared in Jesus. I also had a chance to visit several staff members and the young cook of the castle where I had been a governess. She told me all the latest news of castle life. Later, I was invited to view the castle elegantly decorated for Christmas.

The next two days I had an opportunity to take the train through Salzburg. It appeared like a sleeping town in a fairy tale, with its many cathedral towers standing firmly straight, touched by a dust of snow. The ancient bells of the cathedrals have, for many centuries, called the town's inhabitants to rise and come to worship. The medieval castle on top the mid-town hill appeared immovable and strong, confirming that some things last while others change like the wind. It was a constant reminder that God is our mighty fortress—"Eine Feste Burg," as Martin Luther wrote.

My next visit to family and friends was a highlight all its own. As the train quietly slipped like a sled, through the charming winter scenes of Austria, my mind was flooded again with memories of my past. Again, I was entering the sacred vestibules of my homeland and my roots. Again, I touched the cradle of my childhood.

After the train breezed by my hometown, I came to Attersee, the idyllic lake that by now has become a storehouse of pleasant memories, invoking sweet reflections of the past. On top of one of its hills, I visited my mother's best friend, an academic portrait painter. She had painted us as children, one by one, when we were little and again when we had grown up. She had also painted my mother's portrait and portraits of princesses as well. Her husband, a poet, shared his inspiring poetry with me and, we all exchanged anecdotes of bits and pieces of our common past. Our house had been filled with joy and laughter whenever this friend came to visit my mother and us children.

I also had a chance to visit one of our dearest family friends, Frau Riepl and her daughter Ilse. Frau Riepl had raised four children during the aftermath of the war, and her husband, like my father, had ministered the gospel to countless refugees and local residents. Her love for God, her cheerful eyes and contagious laughter supplied once again a day of sheer plea-sure and joy. That evening she invited me to attend a first-time, historical meeting consisting of all the various Christian denominations and Bible schools. Some of them were the har-vest of her husband's and my father's labor of sowing gospel seeds through Bible studies and evangelism. What an honor it was to share this historic moment with Frau Riepl.

It was hard to leave these heartwarming friends of the olden, golden days of childhood. That was a time that had secured and solidified our family bond, while the world outside was torn asunder. Before I bid farewell, Frau Riepl handed me a bag of Christmas cookies like my mother used to make. They were my companion and comfort, together with the memories they invoked, as the train departed and, once again, carried me from the bosom of my homeland to a foreign world.

In Munich, I rushed to the airport to fly to London where I was to join the Gettys. A limousine brought me and two other employees from the airport to an exclusive hotel, where I stayed the following two weeks. I was enthralled by the exquisite professional service and English food. Again we were served the best cuisine on silver trays in luscious rooms of rare design. After a while, I started imagining the number of hungry people in the world that could be fed by just one of those elegant meals. After a while I became perplexed with the exorbitant wealth and the excessive spending of some of the richest people on earth. How could it be that God would bestow so much on one family, while so many others suffer? The only answer I could find was in Luke 12:48, which says, "To whom much has been given, much is required." This scripture changed my attitude. Daily I pondered the awesome responsibility required of the rich and famous. *Are they heeding the ordinances of God?* I wondered. *Are they carrying out His purposes and fulfilling His plans to bless humanity in Jesus' name?* I was able to resume my attitude of blessing those who are richly endowed and who are called to an awesome task.

Every morning I was driven by limousine to a riverfront house, where the child was staying. I took care of her until dinnertime, occasionally taking long walks along the Thames in the typical London fog. On days off, I had a chance to visit, among other tourist spots, a well known international church on fire for God and the world famous choir in Westminster Abby. God's praises resounded within the walls and ceilings of this magnificent cathedral that was an age old memorial to God.

I was beginning to adjust to this extravagant way of life when, to my horror, I discovered aspects of my employment expectations that directly opposed my personal sense of integrity. I was petrified and prayed to God to give me wisdom and strength. I was faced with choosing between God's law and man's desire—between speaking the truth and keeping silent. In this case, disclosure of the truth was essential. "Therefore to him who knows to do good and does it not, to him it is sin" (James 4:17).

For days I wrestled with the temptation to remain silent in order to ensure my job. This job embodied the potential fulfillment of my dreams and financial security. I could do without eating the fancy meals, sleeping on $5,000 dollars worth of silken sheets, and caring for a child in a room full of splendid Turkish furniture with inlaid ivory and crystal mirrors. But to part with my dreams was another question. I felt temptation knocking at my heart, choking me, enslaving me with shackles made of gold, imprisoning my soul. I prayed for days and finally realized that God had already given me the power to escape temptation. All that I had to do was choose. It was a choice between trust in God and trust in man—between integrity and gold. I had to choose between God's law and the foolish ways of men who are birthed in rebellion and in disregard of the ordinances of God.

But this choice required a price, the painful loss of this employment. By God's grace I had the power to choose what I knew to be the right thing to do. It did cost me my job. It was like being punished for upholding the truth. Then, in the course of the painful loss of this employment, my temptation was to curse them all; but God distinctly said, "Bless, and curse not."

Back at Mary's house I still struggled fiercely with my loss. I tried to gain some strength and courage by studying the temptations Christ endured. After enduring various temptations in the wilderness, Jesus commanded, "Away with you, Satan! For it is written, 'You shall worship the Lord your God, and Him only shall you serve'"(Matt. 4:10-11). Jesus was fighting "fire with fire," as He declared the written Word of God in response to Satan's temptation. In view of the fact that I had chosen to stand on my principles while jeopardizing and eventually losing earthly financial security, I was indeed comforted and strengthened by Jesus' example of overcoming temptation. After fasting for forty days and forty nights, He declared in Matthew 4:4, "It is written, 'Man shall not live by bread alone, but by every word that proceeds from the mouth of God.'"

This word sparked a new vision within me. It restored hope and courage in my heart and began to melt away my bitterness, anxiety and disappointment. As I trusted in His Word, God's holy fire slowly burned away the stubble and thorns in my soul, making a new path for me to follow in the midst of the jungles of this life. This enabled me to bless and be blessed. Slowly, I found new blossoms appearing in my heart, as refreshing springs of Living Water gently permeated the deserts of my soul. As my temporary earthly pleasures and securities had momentarily faded away, I felt privileged to know and grow in the knowledge of Christ, the Living Word, in whose presence there are provisions, joys and pleasures that last into eternity, and that far exceed the temporary pleasures of the world.

> Therefore my heart is glad, and my glory rejoices;
> My flesh also will rest in hope...
> You will show me the path of life;
> In your presence there is fullness of joy;
> At your right hand are pleasures forevermore.
> —PSALM 16:9, 11

> Therefore the children of men put their trust under the
>   shadow of Your wings.
> They are abundantly satisfied with the fullness of your
>   house,
> And you give them drink from the river of your pleasures.
> —PSALM 36:7–8

In view of God's immeasurable eternal pleasures, the fading earthly pleasures seem insignificant and at times foolish. Yet we struggle daily to overcome the temptations of diverse pleasures that are rooted in unbelief, greed or lust, rather than in the love of God.

There are grim warnings regarding man's indulgence in excessive pleasures:

> But know this, that in the last times perilous times will
> come: For men will be lovers of themselves, lovers of
> money... unholy, unloving... despisers of good... lovers
> of pleasures rather than lovers of God.
> —2 TIMOTHY 3:1–4

Come now, you rich, weep and howl for your miseries
that are coming upon you! Your riches are corrupted, and
your garments are moth-eaten. Your gold and silver are
corroded, and their corrosion will be a witness against
you and will eat your flesh like fire. You have heaped up
treasures in the last days . . . You have lived on the earth in
pleasure and luxury, you have fattened your hearts in the
day of slaughter.

—JAMES 5:1–3, 5

Now the parable is this: The seed is the word of God . . .
But the ones on the rock are those who when they hear,
receive the word with joy, and these have no root, who
believe for a while and in time of temptation fall away.
And the ones that fell among thorns are those who when
they have heard, go out and are choked with cares, riches,
and pleasures of life, and bring no fruit to maturity. But the
ones that fell on good ground are those who having heard
the word with a noble and good heart, keep it and bear
fruit with patience.

—LUKE 8:11, 13, 15

When God speaks, are we listening? Are we willing to forego
certain earthly pleasures in order to experience the abundant
pleasure inherent in God's presence? Are we willing, in our voyage through life, to forsake certain earthly securities or temporary pleasures of sin, as Moses did, to be an instrument of
deliverance for a harvest of souls?

By faith Moses, when he became of age, refused to be called
the son of Pharaoh's daughter, choosing rather to suffer
affliction with the people of God that to enjoy the passing
pleasures of sin, esteeming the reproach of Christ greater
riches than the treasures in Egypt, for he looked to the
reward. By faith, he forsook Egypt, not fearing the wrath of
the king; for he endured as seeing HIM who is invisible.

—HEBREWS 11:24–27

63

Are we willing to forsake the bondage and temptations of Egypt in our hearts to find deliverance and healing in God's Kingdom of love and holiness? When we pray the Lord's prayer, "...Lead us not into temptation..." are we allowing God to speak to us and to show us His path of righteousness? God has provided us a way to escape temptation and sin, for He is the "Way, the Truth and the Life" (John 14:6).

> For we do not have an high priest who cannot sympathize with our weakness, but was in all points tempted as we are, yet without sin. Let us therefore come boldly to the throne of grace, that we may obtain mercy and find grace to help in time of need.
>
> —HEBREWS 4:15-16

CHAPTER 9

ANSWER BY FIRE

I N THE COURSE of our journey through life we are continually faced with making decisions and choosing the path on which to travel. When we choose to follow God's plan for our lives, He reveals His plan for us on a daily basis and manifests His care and provision as we trust in Him. When we answer His call to follow Him, God responds to our prayers.

During our upbringing, most of us who were taught how to pray learned to pray by talking to God. We learned how to thank Him for His plentiful supply. We learned how to present lists of various needs or desires accompanied by requests to have them met as speedily as possible. In so doing, we often think we follow Jesus' wonderful example of how we should pray. Those who have had the opportunity to learn the Lord's Prayer may take great interest in the latter part of this prayer that Jesus taught us. With great fervor we may follow its example, as it presents basic human needs to an omnipotent God. However, often unintentionally or unknowingly, we skim over or altogether skip the first part of the Lord's Prayer as described in Matthew:

> Our Father in heaven, Hallowed be Your name. Your kingdom come. Your will be done, on earth as it is in heaven. Give us this day our daily bread. And forgive us our debts,

> As we forgive our debtors. And do not lead us into tempta-
> tion, but deliver us from the evil one. For Yours is the king-
> dom and the power and the glory forever. Amen.
>
> —MATTHEW 6:9-13

In this prayer, several significant facts are established in the first two sentences. They take preeminence to the consequent requests and provide the proper conditions for the latter part of the prayer to be fulfilled. First of all, the fact that there is a God who has the characteristic of a father is acknowledged. Secondly, a relationship and a decree of belonging is identified in the word, "our." It implies that the one praying has accepted the provision available and the conditions necessary to be a child of the Heavenly Father by claiming the forgiving grace made possible by His Son's death for our sins. It also implies that the one praying acknowledges the need for our Heavenly Father, for His provision and protection. Moreover, it implies a commitment to honor and obey. This commitment is further intensified by the subsequent expression of worship, " . . . hallowed be Your name." Within the first few words of the Lord's model prayer, we evolve from acknowledging an intimate relationship with our Heavenly Father to honoring and worshiping the God of the universe whose name is holy—whose name is I AM.

The following statements, "Your kingdom come, Your will be done" reiterate a desire and commitment to acknowledge the rulership of God and to surrender to His authority, His plans and leadership. Only then can we expect and claim our inheritance, as children of God, to be provided for and to be empowered to fulfill His purposes. Only then can we move on to the latter part of the Lord's Prayer and request God's provision, guidance, forgiveness and deliverance. In order for us to pray properly we need to hear God speak to us before we speak to Him. We need to accept His offer to call us His own. We need to accept His love and provision for an intimate relationship with Him. We need acknowledge and surrender to His authority, and we need to heed His Word. Are we listening? Or are we too busy talking to God to hear Him speak? The answer to the question, "When we speak is God listening?" is often in direct proportion to the answer of the question, "When God speaks am I listening?"

In the Lord's Prayer, Jesus first leads us, as mediator between us and God, to our Creator. He boldly assures us of our entrance into the family of God and of belonging to God our Heavenly Father. Then He leads us, as our High Priest, to worship the Lord Most High in the Holiest of Holies. As King of Kings, Jesus leads us to God's throne to surrender to His will and to function in His kingdom. Finally, He leads us, like a true shepherd, to green pastures as a respite from everyday struggles. He also leads us to the Heavenly Father, the source of our physical and spiritual sustenance, restoration and deliverance. It is a prayer of God's design. It is a prayer that addresses basic human requirements and needs. It teaches us to implore and expect God's divine intervention upon our earthly matters in response to our surrender to Him. According to Christ's profound model prayer, our prayer ought to be a response to His call to belong to Him, to worship His holy name, to surrender to His power and will and to trust in His love and grace, deliverance and provision.

When we pray according to God's design, some circumstances in life seem to be readily aligned with the provisions, promises and purposes of God, our Heavenly Benefactor. However, certain circumstances in life call for dramatic intervention in order for God's deliverance to be made manifest.

I related earlier my employment at the handicapped children's home in Southern California. While there I contracted hepatitis. It had passed from child to child and eventually to the staff. I was the last one to be afflicted with it. While I was in the hospital bed praying, God filled the whole room with

His glorious presence and baptized my soul with the Holy Ghost fire.

> He will baptize you with the Holy Spirit and fire.
> —MATTHEW 3:11

It was like a cloud of fire hovering over my room. My heart and soul were aglow like a light bulb. I was on no medication or drugs of any kind. I would play the auto harp and sing praises to God to the great delight of the nurses, visitors and other patients. For several weeks I searched the Scriptures to confirm my experience and to learn of the various functions, forms and purposes of the fire of God. It was to be an intriguing and profound new aspect of my walk with the Lord in the following years of the voyage of my life.

The first Scripture I found was, "For the Lord your God is a consuming fire, a jealous God" (Deuteronomy 4:24). That verse confirmed to me my powerful experience as being in line with God's Word. As I continued my study on the fire of God, I came upon the following verse " . . . for He is a holy God. He is a jealous God . . . " (Joshua 24:19). *What an awesome statement,* I thought, *simply awesome.* Yet it seemed to describe what I was experiencing at that time. There was holiness all around and a spiritual essence with attributes similar to that of fire. As I continued my search in the Scriptures I came upon a passage in Zephaniah.

> But the whole land shall be devoured by the fire of His jealousy.
> —ZEPHANIAH 1:18

This Scripture made me think of a husband very much in love with his bride but in a jealous rage over her unfaithfulness. I realized for the first time how intensely God feels about our unfaithfulness to Him. Our sin is a state and act of rebellion and betrayal—a form of adultery that separates us from Him and that destroys our union with Him. God is jealous for our union and fellowship with *Him*. He yearns for us to know Him and His love. His desire is so great that He sent His only begotten Son to pay the price for our restoration as rightful heirs.

The next Scripture I found on this quest regarding the fire of God was, "'Is not My word like a fire?' says the Lord . . . " (Jeremiah 23:29).

What else can fire do?, I asked myself. I reminisced about the various campfires I had observed in my youth and remembered the warmth of fire as it emanated and lit up people's faces and the area immediately around it. I thought of the moon and the stars and of the sun, an explosive ball of fire. They light up the dark sky and provide direction on our voyage in everyday life. God's Word is like a torch that guides us, as vessels of God, across the sea of life, to safely reach His Kingdom and eternal life with Him.

> Your word is a lamp to my feet
> And a light to my path.
>
> —PSALM 119:105

When God speaks, are we following the path that is lit up by His Word, or do we perish in the darkness and sink into the sea of sin and eternal separation from God? Jesus is our lighthouse. He has set the course of our salvation to safely guide us to eternal life with Him. When God lights the way, do we follow?

Another attribute of fire I found was its comforting and healing power. Likewise, the fire of God in my life seemed to have similar effects. His Word manifested itself as a comforting and healing fire.

> I am the Lord who heals you.
>
> —EXODUS 15:26

On one of my traveling days while I was visiting California's beautiful Lake Tahoe, my skirt got caught on the front seat of my car. Unaware, I stepped out of my van, flipped and crashed onto the pavement with my shoulder taking the brunt of the impact. I was in great pain. I happened to be on the way to a Kathryn Kuhlman meeting in Sacramento. During the service Miss Kuhlman announced, "God wants to heal someone's shoulder. All those with a shoulder problem stand up." I stood up in great anticipation of what God would do. Within minutes, I felt a warm soothing glow like a shimmering fire permeate my arm and shoulder, totally restoring its full use and well-being.

One other day, my friend Lisé came to greet me. As we embraced, she felt a hot, but comforting fire flow through her stomach. "Oh Traudi," she exclaimed, "my stomach is healed!"

Concerned, I replied, "Oh, did you have a stomachache?"

"No," she said, "I've had terrific pain from ulcers for several months; it's all gone now—praise the Lord!"

Occasionally, healing attributes of the Holy Ghost fire would occur during anointed music. That happened to me while someone was singing God's praises; I was instantly healed of a bad cold. In turn, other people experienced the Holy Ghost glow during my anointed instrumental music or singing, while their hearts were stirred and their souls were healed.

One winter, I was in great distress while driving through Pennsylvania in my van. It was nighttime and my heater had broken down; my fingers went numb and my whole body was shivering. I had difficulty holding the wheel. I cried to the Lord, who answered by a hot flow of his healing fire throughout my whole body. At the same time I was overflowing with His joy. This miracle enabled me to keep on driving until I came to a town that provided accommodations and repair. Within minutes, I was able to share this miracle and pray with a young teenage boy who was on his way home to his cancer-stricken mother.

One of the greatest healings we can receive is the healing of our heart. God is a holy fire, but He is also love. His fire is a fire of love and compassion that burns away hostility and strife and replaces it with goodness and grace. When our hearts burn with the fire of God's love, we are energized and transformed into His likeness. We become vessels of healing and instruments of restoring relationships between God and man and between each other.

The fire of God's love in our hearts can transform us and change the course of another person's life. One example was an incident that occurred in the orphanage in New York State where I was working as a counselor. One day, my brand new warm blankets were stolen. They were the only blankets I owned at the time, and I had saved to be able to buy them. I felt violated and victimized for several days, fuming with frustration, anger and revenge. Finally, I prayed. I prayed for God to convict the person's heart to repent and to bring me back to my blankets. But the more I prayed, the more I, myself, was convicted. I saw my own heart in violation of God's love and mercy. *What if that person desperately needed a blanket?* I thought. As my heart stood convicted, I asked God to change my violent attitude on the whole matter. I burst into tears as I repented. My heart and soul were filled with a burning compassion for the intruder. I fasted and prayed for two days. My concern for my blankets faded, and my burden for the culprit's soul grew.

Soon the blankets were mysteriously found in someone's basement. When the thief was discovered, it turned out to be a shy little six-year-old boy in the orphanage. He had been abandoned at home and sent to our care a year earlier. He was an unassuming, well behaved boy, but afflicted with kleptomania that neither he nor anyone else was able to control. When I went to see him, I gently asked if he needed the blankets, and I offered to give them to him. He said he had enough blankets and didn't know why he took them. I invited him to a pizza place for lunch, gave him a little Bible and told him of Jesus' love for him and how He bore our sins on the cross to forgive us and make us whole again. This little boy was mesmerized by the kindness of my actions, the compassion in my heart and the story of Jesus' love. We prayed, and he accepted Jesus into his heart. To my enormous joy and satisfaction, I later learned that he had completely stopped stealing and had become one of the best students in class.

It was God's fire of love that had changed my heart. It enabled this child who was more precious than silver or gold to thrive in His care. The fire of God's love had burnt away my hostility and revenge and replaced them with compassion and concern. Recalling the change in my heart during this entire incident later confirmed to me, together with many other occurrences, the reality of the purifying power of the fire of God and the Scriptures that evoke this vital element of the Holy Spirit.

> For he is a like a refiner's fire and like fullers' soap. He will sit as a refiner and a purifier of silver; He will purify the sons of Levi, and purge them as gold and silver, that they may offer to the Lord an offering in righteousness.
>
> —MALACHI 3:2-3

Another aspect of the purifying and cleansing characteristics of God's fire can be seen and experienced in everyday circumstances. It is the fire that comes by way of hardships and trials. Unfortunately, in our culture today and in the stubbornness of our hearts, this form of soul searching and soul purging is often rejected, avoided and explained away. Yet, in the Bible, the written Word clearly states:

> In this you greatly rejoice, though now for a little while, if need be, you have been grieved by various trials, that the genuineness of your faith, being much more precious than gold that perishes, though it is tested by fire, may be found to praise, honor, and glory at the revelation of Jesus Christ.
>
> —1 PETER 1:6-7

It is in our trials that our faith intensifies, that our love widens and our trust in God deepens. In the face of adversity, we stand bare, shedding our power and control, our rebellion and idolatry and our pride and prejudices. When we let go of our old wineskins, God can pour in the new wine. Only then can we allow God to clothe us with the mantle of His glory and grace. We must allow God to walk with us through the fire of adversity, to cleanse our souls in the midst of the fiery trials, and make us pliable like steel softened in seething temperatures. Then our hearts will sparkle like jewels in God's hand and reflect His radiant love and majesty.

Another fascinating and empowering attribute of God's fire that I discovered in this study was the positive aspect of the destructive force of fire:

> The sight of the glory of the Lord was like a consuming fire on the top of the mountain in the eyes of the children of Israel.
>
> —EXODUS 24:17

> The mountains will melt under Him, and the valleys will split Like wax before the fire, Like waters poured down a steep place.
>
> —MICAH 1:4

> For our God is a consuming fire.
>
> —HEBREWS 12:29

These statements were perplexing and somewhat unsettling at first. It wasn't until I happened to come across a scientific program on television which presented the possibility of the earth's volcanic forces erupting violently in the distant future on earth and under the sea. It was suggested that, during this episode, the earth would be consumed by fire. However, like after a forest fire, the earth and its natural growths would consequently be renewed and replenished.

These are the positive effects of fire's destructive power. I realized that the process of purification was really a process of destruction and renovation, whether it occurs in nature or in the voyage of our souls. Our hearts and minds are like fertile soil that holds roots and seeds of a potential harvest. Are we harboring the seeds of God's Word that will bear His fruit and produce everlasting life? Are we allowing the fire of the Holy Spirit to destroy the thorns and briars of wickedness in our hearts and renew our souls to bear the fruit that reflects His glory and love?

The destructive forces of fire also contain the capacity to protect. I had never understood what the phrase, "Fight fire with fire" really meant, until I saw a blazing forest fire in Southern California. Within several days firefighters, volunteers and construction workers had surrounded the burning forest with a circle of fire. By the time the advancing fire had reached the circle, it had nowhere else to travel and all the surrounding inhabitants, animals and fields were safe. Likewise, God surrounds us with a circle of His fire. He surrounds us with His Word and His angels—and by His people. Like natural fire warding off deadly beasts, God's Word and holy fire protect us from various kinds of onslaught and attack. Much like a circle of burning oil surrounding a vessel on the sea to ward off enemy ships, God's protective fire surrounds us. It wards off the fiery darts of Satan that cannot prosper because God is our shield.

> For You, O Lord, will bless the righteous;
> With favor You will surround him as with a shield.
> —PSALM 5:12

> For the Lord God is a sun and shield;
> The Lord will give grace and glory;
> No good thing will He withhold
> From those who walk uprightly.
> —PSALM 84:11

You are my hiding place and my shield;
I hope in Your word.

—PSALM 119:114

As God's Word, shield and holy fire ward off our assailants, God also pursues His enemies. Since God is a consuming fire and His Word is like a fire, when God speaks the enemy flees.

"Is not My word like a fire?" says the Lord, "and like a hammer that breaks the rock in pieces?"

—JEREMIAH 23:29

A fire goes before Him,
And burns up all His enemies round about.

—PSALM 97:3

So it was, whenever the ark set out, that Moses said, "Rise up, O Lord! Let Your enemies be scattered, and let those who hate You flee before You."

—NUMBERS 10:35

As the fire burns the woods,
And as the flame sets the mountains on fire,
So pursue them with Your tempest,
And frighten them with Your storm.

—PSALM 83:14–15

When God speaks, are we listening and setting the enemy to flight? Do we rise up, in Jesus' name, like a roaring lion, to confound the enemy?

A lady walking to a church meeting one evening encountered two men who tried to rob and assault her. She held up her Bible and started preaching. All of a sudden, they ran away at high speed. To her great astonishment, at the end of the week, she saw the same two men giving their testimony of having received Christ as their Savior. After the meeting, she asked them, "Do you remember me? Whatever made you run so fast so suddenly?"

They replied, "Lady, didn't you know? There were two large

angels standing behind you with swords of fire in their hands!"

During a worship service in Los Angeles one evening, a group of hoodlums walked in from the streets, disturbing the meeting for twenty minutes. Nobody dared to confront them, so I quietly commanded the demons to depart in Jesus' name. At that instant the whole group got up and hurriedly walked out the door.

God pursues His enemies. When He, our Captain, speaks, are we listening? As His army, when He commands us, are we heeding His command and putting the enemy to flight by His Word and fire?

At times in my journey through life, my verbal use of God's Word and of the name of Jesus have warded off verbal, emotional or physical assaults. Let me share the following example: Almost a decade after the painful departure from my fiancé, I married a Christian man with great hopes for creating a godly home. But all my dreams were soon shattered. The man I married began to exhibit tendencies that had been hidden during our courtship. Those tendencies surfaced in the form of verbal and physical assaults, and ultimately destroyed our marriage. On one occasion, in a fit of rage, he tried to strangle me by jerking me by my neck to the ground. I exclaimed, "Jesus, help!" Instantly, this violent man loosened his grip.

The name of Jesus is the name above all names! To Him every knee shall bow, and every mouth confess that He is Lord. His name is a fire that cannot be quenched, because He is the Word of God. He is a holy fire that causes darkness to flee and wickedness to be devoured.

> Our God shall come, and shall not keep silent;
> A fire shall devour before Him!
>
> —PSALM 50:3

Another purpose of the fire of God is to be a testimony of God's existence, power and holiness. Its purpose is also to call people to repentance—to turn from idolatry and rebellion, and commit to serving and worshiping Him. When King Abaziah of Samaria inquired of Baal-Zebub, the god of Ekron, whether he would recover from an injury, the angel of the Lord said to Elijah, "Arise, go up to meet the messengers of the King of Samaria, and say to them . . . you shall surely die" (2 Kings 1:3,4). When the king sent a captain of fifty men to him, twice, Elijah answered each time, "'If I am a man of God, then let fire come down from heaven and consume you and your fifty men.' And fire came down from heaven and consumed him and his fifty" (2 Kings 1:10).

Another time, when Ahab was king over Israel, Elijah admonished him, saying,

> . . . you have forsaken the commandments of the Lord, and you have followed the Baals.
> —1 Kings 18:18

Then Elijah challenged Ahab's people to bring a burnt offering and said,

> I alone am left a prophet of the Lord; but Baal's prophets are four hundred and fifty men . . . choose one bull . . . but put no fire under it . . . Then you call on the name of your gods, and I will call on the name of the Lord; and the God who answers by fire, He is God.
> —1 Kings 18:22–24

> So they took the bull which was given them, . . . and called on the name of Baal from morning even 'til noon, . . . But there was no voice, no one answered . . . Then with the stones he built an altar in the name of the Lord, . . . and said, "Lord God of Abraham, Isaac and Israel, let it be known this day that you are God in Israel, and that I am Your servant, . . . Hear me, O Lord, hear me, that this people may know that You have turned their hearts back to You again." Then the fire of the Lord fell and consumed the burnt sacrifice . . .

> Now when all the people saw it, they fell on their faces; and
> they said, "The Lord, He is God! The Lord, He is God!"
> —1 KINGS 18:26, 32, 36-39

First, Elijah acknowledged God and stated his own unwaver-
ing service to Him. Next, he implored God, who then
answered by fire, to reveal Himself to His people, in order to
turn their hearts back to Him. At that time, Elijah proved himself to be a man who acknowledged, worshiped and served
God, and who exhibited extraordinary faith and obedience for
the sake of a whole nation. He stood alone in the midst of an
idolatrous people and risked his life to be instrumental in
turning their hearts back to God.

When we pray, do we first acknowledge God as Lord of our
lives? When we pray, are we willing to stand alone in worshiping and serving Him? Are we willing to be an instrument of
restoration and repentance for others who need to return to
God? When we pray, do we ask God to help us accomplish our
own plans, or to manifest His magnificent power and plans in
our lives? Do we pray to a silent god of our imagination or to
the God who answers by fire?

When we pray, are we ready and willing to be consumed by
the fire of His Word? Sometimes the most dramatic changes
that need to occur in our lives are changes within our own
hearts and minds. How fortunate we are to have access to God
our Father, who is not silent, but who answers. He is the God
who answers by fire—the fire of His Word, the fire of His love
and the fire of the Holy Spirit.

Nevertheless, not all of God's answers take form in tremendous external manifestations of fire, but, as mentioned in previous chapters, also in the still small voice of the Lord. That
may occur in our everyday lives today, just as it has occurred
throughout many centuries to various individuals and groups
of people.

And behold, the Lord passed by, and a great and strong wind tore into the mountains and broke the rocks in pieces before the Lord, but the Lord was not in the wind, and after the wind an earthquake, but the Lord was not in the earthquake; And after the earthquake a fire, but the Lord was not in the fire; and after the fire a still small voice.

—1 Kings 19:11-12

PART II

JOURNEY OF
THE HEART AND MIND

CHAPTER 10

JOURNEY BACK TO GOD

THROUGHOUT THE COURSE of our lives, our hearts and minds experience a journey all their own. It is the voyage of our inner being. It is a voyage in which God seeks to reveal Himself and guide us into His presence in everyday life. No matter how pleasant or how treacherous life may be, the path that is forged by the hand of God, in the deepest valleys or on the highest mountaintops, is the path that engages us in an intimate, personal relationship with our Creator.

On the way to our final destination of life after death, we may stray far from the road that leads to an encounter with God who knows us by name. During our pursuit of various goals in our lives, God is calling us to embark on an inner voyage from the kingdom of darkness in the absence of Christ to eternal life in His presence, glory and grace. The depth of His grace and power of His Word carry us across the sea of hopelessness and vanity to the shores of His kingdom. The journey back to God is not always a smooth ride. It is even a treacherous one at times. But the grace of God faithfully ensures a safe passage for His children from the bondage of sin and unbelief to freedom in the presence of the Most High God. He is relentlessly beckoning and drawing us to experience His love in a relationship with Him. He is a loving Father, friend and king. Even in the midst of life's bitter grief and pain, it is possible for us to experience the pleasure of His love, peace and joy. He promised to give us abundant life. It is in Him alone that we can find it.

> In Your presence is fullness of joy;
> At Your right hand are pleasures forevermore.
> —PSALM 16:11

> And those who seek me diligently will find me.
> —PROVERBS 8:17

> He is a rewarder of those who diligently seek Him.
> —HEBREWS 11:6

When we seek God diligently He rewards us with His forgiveness and love and a personal relationship with Him. But when our hearts and minds wander away from a relationship with God, even as believers, we can find ourselves in painful, dark and desolate places of the soul. Whether we are distracted by trials, or lured away by worldly success, pride and ungodly pleasures, we inevitably allow our souls to wander into a spiritual desert. Often we're not aware of those desolate places in our hearts. We may thrive for a time on a series of mirages of false hopes, beliefs and dreams until we realize that we're hopelessly lost, wandering aimlessly, and dying of hunger and thirst. Like a Babylon within ourselves, we may be building and indulging in our own idolatrous castles of success and pleasures until we are hopelessly faced with sudden destruction. We may passionately pursue various carnal endeavors until we find ourselves drifting into volatile situations of jealous rage and betrayal.

How far do we have to stray before we realize that we are lost? How severely endangered and in pain do we have to be before we are willing to seek the path that was ordained for us to travel? These questions pertain to us as individuals, families, communities and nations.

Why do we go astray? Why do we jeopardize our lives to taste the temporary pleasure of self will? Whatever the reason that we wander away from God in our everyday life, God is watching and waiting for us to return to Him. He is calling us by name. Do we hunger and thirst to know Him? Do we long for His presence in our lives? God has given His utmost to find us and to bring us back into His kingdom. Do we hunger and thirst for His love enough to give Him our utmost? In His presence He has set before us a banqueting table, a feast abounding with His love, wisdom, beauty and strength. He has provided a thirst quenching drink, the pure water of His own vineyard, the blood of His own Son Jesus Christ, that was shed for the forgiveness of our sins. He provided a ransom that enables us to gain entrance into His presence to feast and to fellowship with Him.

> . . . and truly our fellowship is with the Father and with His Son Jesus Christ.
>
> —1 JOHN 1:3

> Come, eat of my bread
> And drink of the wine I have mixed.
>
> —PROVERBS 9:5

> But whoever drinks of the water that I shall give Him will never thirst.
>
> —JOHN 4:14

As we fellowship with Him, we feast in His glory and grace, and drink of His river of perfect peace and joy. The fellowship we have with other believers who walk in communion with Him is incomparable to the fleeting pleasures of this world. The ultimate pleasure is to find God and to delight in His people as He delights in us. When His love and fire burn in our hearts and minds, our souls are satisfied by the pleasure of His presence.

> For the Lord takes pleasure in His people.
>
> —PSALM 149:4

The Lord takes pleasure in those who fear Him,
In those who hope in His mercy.

—PSALM 147:11

They are abundantly satisfied with the fullness at Your
house,
And You give them drink from the river of Your pleasures.

—PSALM 36:8

CHAPTER 11

PEACE, BE STILL

IT WAS DAWN, one day in February 1996. Snow had blanketed the Colorado earth, as the sky faintly blushed in the early morning rays. Softly descending snowflakes whispered blessings of peace upon creation. For a moment, I stood in awe of this delicate, pristine landscape, shaped by the hand of God. A holy hush enveloped the fields, and the pale purple mountains rose in standing ovation to honor God's majesty and splendor.

The slowly approaching sunrise bathed the hills in a soft glow as if to view the world through rose-colored glasses. The peace of these moments was profound. It commands my body, mind and soul to stay still and ponder God's silence, which, at that moment, seemed to speak louder than any word I had ever heard. My heart was gripped with an attitude of listening as a hush came over my soul, and the anchor of God's peace descended deep into my spirit. His peace held steadfast my unsettled thoughts. My emotions had been thrashed around like a vessel tossed, once again, by unexpected winds.

For weeks my mind had been in turmoil over the loss of a good job that had embodied new hope for my dreams to come true. My hope and trust for fulfilling my dreams were rooted in the job and not in the Lord. My heart was raging like a ship about to capsize, while my lips tasted the venom of hostility, fear and defeat. I was battling another storm in the voyage of my life, but this time the storm was raging entirely inside of me.

It wasn't until the whisper of this glorious winter morning compelled me to seek the Master's face, the Captain of my "ship," that I recaptured some composure. The anchor of His Word and peace regained control over the tempest of my soul. When I hearkened, the Savior's still, small voice declared again and again, "Bless, and do not curse" (Romans 12:14). I received those words into my heart and mind like the earth welcomes the gentle rain in springtime to bring forth its blossoms and fruits. As I surrendered to and trusted in God's Word, my heart became enveloped with a profound peace. My heart and mind were slowly transformed, once again, from fear to faith, from wickedness to wisdom. I realized, again, the glorious inheritance we have in Christ Jesus. The eternal wealth that is found in His Word and in His presence cannot be compared with all the wealth in the world.

> But of Him you are in Christ Jesus, who became for us wisdom to God—and righteousness and sanctification and redemption.
>
> —1 CORINTHIANS 1:30

> Happy is the man who finds wisdom,
> And the man who gains understanding;
> For her proceeds are better than profits of silver,
> And her gain than fine gold.
> She is more precious than rubies,
> And all things you may desire cannot compare with her.
> Length of days is in her right hand,
> In her left hand riches and honor.
> Her ways are ways of pleasantness,
> And all her paths are peace.
>
> —PROVERBS 3:13–17

Furthermore, God's wisdom, by the entrance of His Word

into my heart and mind, produced purity and peace, righteousness and mercy. His Word descended into my soul like snow
upon seething volcanic rock and like a woolen fleece upon a
shorn lamb bleating in the cold of winter. As a shepherd gently
leads his sheep to quiet waters, so Jesus leads our souls to the
pastures of His peace, because He, Himself, is our peace.

> And He shall stand and feed His flock . . . and this One
> shall be peace . . . For He Himself is our peace.
> —MICAH 5:4-5; EPHESIANS 2:14

> But the wisdom that is from above is first pure, then
> peaceable, gentle, wiling to yield, full of mercy and good
> fruits, without partiality and without hypocrisy. Now the
> fruit of righteousness is sown in peace by those who
> make peace.
> —JAMES 3:17-18

> For unto us a child is born, unto us a Son is given; and the
> government will be upon His shoulder. And His name will
> be called Wonderful, Counselor, Mighty God, Everlasting
> Father, Prince of Peace.
> —ISAIAH 9:6

It is the greatest gift in life to know and to be known; to
love and to be led by this great Shepherd, who is the Prince of
Peace. It is a gift that cannot be bought by silver or gold. It is
worth more than all the riches in the world. It is a gift that was
paid for in full by the spotless Lamb of God, Jesus our
Shepherd. When Jesus bore our sins on the cross, He became
our righteousness. His forgiveness and cleansing blood
ensured our peace and fellowship with God. As we are
cleansed by the blood of the Lamb, we are covered, as with
feathers of a dove, to rise above the turmoil of our sin within
us as well as the turbulence of the sins in the world. God's
peace and righteousness are inseparable, like two hands
folded in prayer, or two wings of an eagle in flight. When

God clothes us with His righteousness and peace, we can soar like eagles above the turbulent sea of our hearts and minds, and descend like a dove to find rest on quiet grounds.

> For He made Him who knew no sin to be sin for us, that we might become the righteousness of God in Him.
> —2 CORINTHIANS 5:21

> The work of righteousness will be peace, and the effect of righteousness, quietness and assurance forever.
> —ISAIAH 32:17

Furthermore, God's righteousness and peace are not only a gift for us to receive, but they are also a command for us to heed. When Christ offers and commands His righteousness to abide in us, He commands His peace to reside in us. When God speaks, are we listening? Are we heeding His commands and allowing Him to command His peace to reign in our thoughts and hearts?

> And let the peace of God rule in your hearts, to which also you were called in one body; and be thankful.
> —COLOSSIANS 3:15

Sooner or later, our thoughts are going to affect our actions—whether for good or for evil, for war or for peace. "As a man thinketh, so he is . . . " (Proverbs 23:7). When we trust in God and allow His wisdom and righteousness to rule in our hearts and thoughts, our actions will produce God's peace.

> Casting down arguments and every high thing that exalts itself against the knowledge of God, bringing every thought into captivity to the obedience of Christ.
> —2 CORINTHIANS 10:5

> And do not be conformed to this world, but be transformed by the renewing of your mind, that you may prove what is that good and acceptable and perfect will of God.
> —ROMANS 12:2

> You will keep him in perfect peace, whose mind is stayed
> on You, because he trusts in You.
>
> —ISAIAH 26:3

When we allow His Word to command our every thought, the treacherous storms on the voyage of our minds subside. Are we allowing God to command the voyage of our hearts and minds? Are we asking *Him* to still our internal storms? Although God intervenes, and often comes to our rescue, at times, He waits for us to seek Him out. When Jesus and His disciples encountered a violent storm while on board a boat crossing a lake, Jesus waited until He was sought out. Only then, did He rise and command the winds, "Peace, be still!" Jesus was there all along; why did the disciples wait so long to request for Him to save them? Why does it take us so long to seek Him out? He is always there, willing to command His peace in our hearts and minds.

When God rises in our hearts and speaks, are we listening? Do we seek Him out, allowing Him to proclaim, "Peace be still!"? His peace is like a river that never goes dry. Even though, in His mercy, God provides a drink for us from His river of love and peace, He also expects us to turn from our rebellion, forsake the deserts of our soul and actively seek His river of pure joy in His righteousness and peace. Instead of waiting for God's river to come to us, we must pursue it. Are we thirsty enough to run to the river of life, the river of God's righteousness and peace?

> Oh, that you had heeded My commandments! Then your
> peace would have been like a river,
>
> And your righteousness like the waves of the sea.
>
> —ISAIAH 48:18

> Depart from evil and do good;
> Seek peace and pursue it.
>
> —PSALM 34:14

CHAPTER 12

VOLCANO

WHEN MOUNT VESUVIUS erupted in 1904 and 1944, its fire and hot ashes fell upon and destroyed thousands of men, women and children, as well as houses on land and ships in the sea. Fortunately, natural disasters of this magnitude occur only periodically. However, there are thousands of people who are regularly victims of the violent "volcanic outbursts" of anger. This occurs to adults as well as children in various environments but mostly within their own homes.

Some people's anger can set their tongues aflame like active volcanoes.

> The tongue is a fire, a world of iniquity. It is an unruly evil, full of deadly poison. With it we bless our God and Father, and with it we curse men who have been made in the similitude of God.
>
> —JAMES 3:6, 8

> Wrath is cruel and anger a torrent,
> But who is able to stand before jealousy?
>
> —PROVERBS 27:4

Like hot volcanic ash falling on the ships at sea, the words spoken in uncontrolled anger burn deep into unprotected victims' hearts. Unfortunately, many of these victims are children who then bear the scars of these violent outbursts, sometimes throughout a whole lifetime. At times these outbursts can inflict fatal blows or deep wounds that slowly kill the body, mind and soul. The people that are able to escape such treacherous affliction or who are able to heal in time are often a true marvel and a witness to God's grace and healing power.

Many men and women carry into their adulthood the childhood scars of someone's fits of anger. Some are fortunate to have experienced enough healing to present their lives as trophies of God's triumphant power and love. My life has been an example of the disabling injuries and scars of various traumas and the enabling, healing power of God. As I struggled in the course of my voyage through life to overcome the wounds inflicted upon me, both in my childhood and in my adult years, I experienced again and again the miracle power available to us in God's Word.

Sometimes in my own life, people's anger erupted like spits of fire and flaming arrows, and their slander and gossip spread among family, friends and community. The sails of the vessel of my heart and soul caught on fire and slowly disintegrated as I desperately sought rescue and fought for my life. Occasionally pastors, friends and other family members helped me put out the flames that were slowly invading various areas of my soul. It was God's Word of hope, wisdom and love that extinguished the enemy fire at last. Moreover, the diligent prayers and kindness of God's people helped me mend the damaged sails of my soul. When I was prepared to "sail" again, I waited upon God's Word to breathe upon me like a wind to set my "ship a' sail" again. The holy fire of God's Word was rekindled in my soul. Instead of being consumed by enemy fire, the vessel of my heart became ablaze with God's healing fire.

The other face of anger is the righteous anger of the Lord. We are admonished in Psalms 37:8 to "cease from anger and forsake wrath." Yet in Ephesians 4:26 we are advised to "be angry but sin not." This implies that in Christ there is a holy anger that may be exhibited with discretion and discernment of His Word. To have our anger under the power and control of the Holy Spirit is a great attribute to attain.

> He who is slow to anger is better than the mighty.
> And he that rules his spirit than he who takes a city.
> —PROVERBS 16:32

When a volcano erupts and its molten lava flows down and cools, it produces new soil. The new soil then nourishes new growth and provides new land and sustenance for mankind to enjoy. When we are provoked to anger, do we respond righteously or do we explode and heap hot lava of insults upon those around us? Do we allow God to cool our fiery outbursts so that they become new soil and opportunity for fertile ground and new fruit to the glory of God?

One of God's abounding attributes is mercy. In His mercy, He forgives. In His mercy, He heals and restores. In His mercy, He delivers. Furthermore, God, in His mercy, is slow to anger. Nevertheless, even though God is slow to anger, He can be provoked to anger. But God implores us not to provoke Him to anger.

> Because of their wickedness which they have committed to provoke Me to anger, in that they went to burn incense and to serve other gods whom they did not know, they nor you nor your fathers . . .
> —JEREMIAH 44:3

> Behold, the day of the Lord comes, cruel, with both wrath and fierce anger, to lay the land desolate; and He will destroy its sinners from it.
> —ISAIAH 13:9

> Do not go after other gods to serve them and worship them, and do not provoke Me to anger with the works of your hands; and I will not harm you.
> —JEREMIAH 25:6

Additionally, God is also a God of grace and great compassion, and He longs for us to know Him and to restore our relationship with Him. He longs to give us His joy and bless us with forgiveness, favor and life everlasting.

> But He, being full of compassion, forgave their iniquity,
> And did not destroy them.
> Yes, many a time, He turned His anger away,
> And did not stir up all His wrath.
>
> —PSALM 78:38

> For His anger is but for a moment,
> His favor is for life;
> Weeping may endure for a night,
> But joy comes in the morning.
>
> —PSALM 30:5

CHAPTER 13

ICEBERG

OVER THE PAST millennia, an untold number of ocean going vessels have perished by crashing into an iceberg, or by being encircled and trapped by masses of ice.

In the case of the Titanic, the captain had been warned several times to change the course of the ship due to sightings of icebergs. But he insisted on taking the shortest and fastest route to meet arrival deadlines. By heeding his own impulses and disregarding the wise counsel of others, he carried hundreds of people on the fast route to their unexpected final destiny—death.

How many times have we had hunches or warnings from others or from God, Himself, to take another route in our lives? Do we listen to the warning signs?

> A prudent man foresees evil and hides himself,
> But the simple pass on and are punished.
> —PROVERBS 22:3

What are some of the facets of our character that are submerged in our hearts, not easily discovered until we crash to pieces? Is there pride, deceit or stubbornness lurking in the depths of our souls? Do we ignore the warning signs of God's Word urging us to avoid treacherous tendencies that lurk within us?

For from within, out of the heart of men, proceed evil
thoughts.

—MARK 7:21

Whether we are confronted by the icebergs of arrogance,
hostility and hardness of heart in other people, or by the stub-
born blocks of bitterness and deceit in ourselves, we are
warned in God's Word to avoid traveling in their paths.

Do not enter the path of the wicked,
And do not walk in the way of evil.
Avoid it, do not travel on it;
Turn away from it and pass on.

Take firm hold of instruction, do not let go;
Keep her, for she is your life.

—PROVERBS 4:14-15, 13

Let us walk humbly and wisely in the fear and admonition
of the Lord. Let us heed His Word and avoid the death traps of
rebellion and wickedness in our hearts.

After my abusive marriage ended in divorce, my soul was
harboring enormous masses of hostile thoughts and bitter
feelings toward life in general, and God in particular. It seemed
as if the person that had loved Jesus since childhood was suddenly rotting away in bitterness and my heart became frozen
in hostility and despair. In final desperation, I cried to God to
help me in my distress, and to enable me to trust in Him no
matter how bleak life's circumstances were. In response to
this appeal, God spoke to me in a still, small voice and said,
"Because you have done this, I will honor and bless you."

As I was allowing myself to go through the grieving process
of a shattered marriage and the grim prospect of childlessness.
I also remained committed to heal from the physical and emotional damage incurred by the previous abuse. During this
time, I was welcoming again the ever increasing healing

presence of God in my life and basking in the wonder and pleasure of knowing Him. As I slowly gained physical, emotional and spiritual strength, I was able, like an icebreaker in Antarctica, to pierce through the enormous masses of frozen hurt. By trusting Him, the icebergs of hatred and bitterness in my heart melted as I continued my voyage in life. I was able, once again, to testify of God's healing love and to give honor to His name.

CHAPTER 14

SHIPWRECKED

A T TIMES, IN the course of our voyage through life, we encounter turbulent circumstances. Some encounters may be so severe that the damages incurred by them extinguish hope for restoration. Inwardly the vessels of our hearts and souls crash upon the rocks of devastation and despair. Indeed we may lose all capacity to cry out for help, and we simply ask, "God, why have You forsaken me?" The momentary silence seems to last forever but is finally broken when our Heavenly Father mercifully reaches out His hand to deliver us. It is a familiar question—a question that expresses the epitome of our human dilemma, and one that Jesus asked on the cross of Calvary. How did God the Father respond to His Son's cry and perplexity? God answered by raising His Son from death, by crowning Him King of Kings and by giving Him an eternal kingdom to rule.

This kind of dramatic response to a desperate question is part of our inheritance as children of grace. God answers by restoring our hope. God answers by restoring our circumstance. As Jesus called Lazarus to come forth from the tomb, God calls us forth by His resurrection power and commands new life to arise in our being. He commands new life to arise in our minds, our bodies, our emotions, our relationships and our circumstances. He is eager and able, not only to salvage

97

the pieces of broken vessels of our hearts and minds, but He is able to completely rebuild our lives. Through the power of the Holy Spirit, God answers our desperate cry and sets our shipwrecked souls to sail again. Are we allowing God to repair our hearts and minds? Are we submitting our broken pieces to be arranged according to His mercy, wisdom and grace?

While some shipwrecks in our lives may be caused by outward circumstances, some may be caused by our own sin. When we disregard the rulership of Christ in our daily lives and appoint ourselves self-made captains, we engage in a mutiny of the vessel of our souls. Sooner or later, we get off course and become disoriented and defenseless. We may find ourselves stranded in uninhabitable lands, while we sink in the quicksand of temptations. Our vessels rot in rebellion, unrepentant attitudes and self-condemnation. Even then, when we ask, "Has God forsaken us?" God answers by way of the cross of Calvary and the risen Christ. He offers an anchor for the soul and deliverance for our heart.

> We are confident of things . . . that accompany
> salvation . . . This hope we have as an anchor of the soul.
> —HEBREWS 6:9, 19

> Therefore we do not lose heart . . . the inward man is
> being renewed day by day.
> —2 CORINTHIANS 4:16

> "For I will restore health to you, And heal you of your
> wounds," says the Lord.
> —JEREMIAH 30:17

No matter why or how the vessel of our souls goes astray, collapses or is shipwrecked, Jesus, the Master voyager, is there to deliver us. Whether our wounds are self inflicted or caused by circumstances beyond our control, God is our anchor and our hope of restoration. Are we submitting the broken pieces of our shipwrecked hearts and souls to be restored and rear-ranged according to His mercy, wisdom and grace? Are we allowing the blood of the nail-pierced Lamb of God to cleanse us, wash away the stench of death and despair and fill us anew with the fragrance of His holiness, His hope and healing? Are we allowing the Holy Spirit to empower our lives and guide us to the shores of His presence?

CHAPTER 15

ROCK OF AGES

DURING MY FAMILY'S first ocean voyage, the ship we were on stopped several times before its final destination. Each stop was an opportunity for the enormous vessel to refuel, make repairs, replenish the food supply, and allow some seamen the chance to rest. At the same time, it was an opportunity to open the gates for new travelers to board.

In the early morning hours of the day of our arrival in the new land of "opportunities and freedom," the first sign of land was the Statue of Liberty. Gracefully holding high the torch of freedom, she greeted us silently with her posture of dignity and strength. She stood proud and confident upon a small island of rock that every vessel had to pass before entering the harbor of New York. Only within the harbor were the passengers of the ocean liner allowed to disembark and step upon the land of abundance and freedom.

How very much this part of the ocean voyage is like entering the harbor of God's love and freedom, I thought later. Those who will enter in must first pass by the Rock of Ages, His Son Jesus, by whose blood we have gained free access to liberty from the bondage of sin, guilt and eternal death. Through this Rock we have gained access to God's abundant love and the light of His kingdom. Freedom stands upon this Rock. Freedom promises abundant life as it holds up the torch of truth—God's Holy Word.

As we journey through life towards the presence of the Most High God, we stop at various harbors within our hearts to rest, to grow, to be repaired and to be prepared to travel on. As we travel through life, God leads us to various people and experiences that invariably become powerful tools for strength and restoration. They become anchors of faith, lighthouses of hope and horns of wisdom to warn us of treacherous paths. We, in turn, become harbors of His grace and lighthouses of His light to guide others to the Rock of Ages and to introduce them to an encounter with the living God. He is the Master Voyager and Captain of every vessel whose anchor of hope is unmoved.

> We are confident of these things...that accompany
> salvation...This hope we have as an anchor of the soul.
> —HEBREWS 6:9, 19

Let us follow God's light and heed His warning signs. Let us lead others to the safe shores of freedom. Let us obey His commands to forge for us and for many others a path of life and not of destruction. Let us embark on a voyage ordained by God's grace to enable us and many others to discover and inherit the riches of His kingdom. Let us offer up to Him honor and praise for the unspeakable treasures of His glory and love.

> Giving thanks to the Father, who has qualified us to be
> partakers of the inheritance of the saints in the light. He
> has delivered us from the power of darkness and trans-
> lated us into the kingdom of the Son of His love, in whom
> we have redemption through His blood, the forgiveness
> of sins... attaining to all riches of the assurance under-
> standing to the knowledge of the mystery of both the
> Father and of Christ in whom are hidden all the treasures
> of wisdom and knowledge.
> —COLOSSIANS 1:12–14; 2:2–3

> As you have therefore received Christ Jesus the Lord, so
> walk in Him . . . for in Him dwells all the fullness of the
> Godhead bodily; and you are complete in Him, who is the
> head of all principality and power.
>
> —COLOSSIANS 2:6, 9-10

Christ died for us and rose again so that we may enter into the presence of the Father, safely passing from the kingdom of darkness to the kingdom of light in Him. God has ordained our lives to be a voyage to His presence. In the harbor of His presence we can have fellowship with Him, claim our inheritance of eternal life and partake of the glory of His power and love. God also ordained our lives to be a voyage in His service, a living testimony and monument of His mercy and grace. He wants our testimonies to inspire others to experience the pleasure of His presence and to inherit the immeasurable splendor and treasures of His kingdom. Let us offer ourselves to be instruments of His hand to rescue and to enable others to embark upon the voyage ordained by His grace. Let us help them to reach the Rock of Ages, to enter the harbor of God's presence and to partake of the treasures of God's kingdom.

We cannot change the direction and power of the wind, but we can adjust the sails to be empowered by its force. Let us set the sails of our souls in the right direction to escape eternal death and to be empowered by the glory and grace of God. Let us allow the Holy Spirit to empower us like a mighty wind or, at times, like a gentle breeze, to become vessels in His service and trophies of His majesty and grace.

CHAPTER 16

LIGHTHOUSE

I N THE SUMMER of 1998, I had the great privilege of returning to Newport, Rhode Island. During a week of scorching temperatures all over the United States, I sought refuge in the cool winds of the rocky shore. I climbed over a wooded hill to reach certain rocks that harbored a lighthouse. As I gazed into the distant horizon, I saw, to my delight and surprise, a fleet of sailboats approaching. I stood in awe as I watched hundreds of them from various nations, mostly attired in white, but some in red, orange or blue. As they came closer and closer, I realized that the whole fleet was engaged in a race, pressing toward the goal—the harbor. By the time the boats reached the waters near the tip of the island where I enthusiastically observed them, I heard exuberant shouts coming from the ships entering the entrance of the harbor. I waved happily to them as my heart vibrated in their joy and my voice echoed their triumph.

What an inspiring event this was for me. I couldn't help thinking of our Savior's profound joy when He sees each of us, His children, His vessels, press toward the goal and victoriously enter the safe harbor of His presence. He is calling us to press forward with this sacred goal in mind—to see Him face to face. As we journey through life, we see Him only as through a glass darkly. Yet through His Comforter, the Holy Spirit, we may come into His presence with thanksgiving.

Within a couple of hours of such heavenly musing, the winds died down as the setting sun turned water and sky into a banquet of scarlet wine. Soon, a hush came over the evening sky. The water, now slowly rising with the tide, faded to a smooth silver blue, like a satin sheet being pulled towards the earth, ready to succumb to slumber. I decided to drive to the other side of the island to watch the moon rise. I stopped at the Breaker mansion. From inside its gilded halls came the distinguished sounds of pianists and opera singers offering their talents during the summer music festival. With one ear listening to the music and the other to gentle ocean waves, I waited for the moon. It finally arose like a fireball emerging from the depths of the dark sea. As it majestically climbed the star sprinkled ceiling of the black sky, it seemed to generously pour a bucket of pure gold upon the earth's velvet nighttime covering, the midnight sea.

What splendor there is at night or day, I thought. God has set the sun by day and the moon, like a lighthouse in the night, to guide the way on our earthly travels. God manifests even greater splendor as He, Himself, like a lighthouse, guides our way to the harbor of His presence and warns us of treacherous paths. When winds are howling and the nights and days are filled with menacing clouds or fog, we sometimes cannot see His light or hear His warning signals. But His hand is there to guide us, to protect us and to lead us on.

FROM SHAME TO RESTORATION

ONE OF THE roughest and most adverse obstacles on the way to the believer's goal is shame. Shame is born out of the depravity of the human heart and often leads us into a treacherous and trying path. It can misguide, discourage, incapacitate and even kill. Shame is a direct consequence of man's sin and the inevitable product of our separation from God.

First of all, there is the shame of our sin. Secondly, there is shame that can be induced by the sin of others—even Satan himself. How many times a minute are men, women and children around the world abused, abandoned or slowly killed by continual bouts of shame inflicted by another human being. It is a way of being cursed, rather than blessed. Often it can leave permanent scars on the heart and mind of the one victimized by it.

Living in a world where sin runs rampant, we are continually surrounded and often assaulted by people's words and actions that are intended to hurt and shame us. It is a lifelong struggle to ward off, heal from and guard our hearts from the deadly wounds of fiery darts of shame. They can come across our daily lives in our homes and workplaces, in our communities and among our fellow believers. To add to the ongoing conflict of living in a fallen world, our own sin and unbelief contribute to our sometimes tumultuous voyage in life. As the world and Satan, himself, can inflict wounds by onslaughts of shame, our own sin can lead us onto a treacherous path of shame and worthlessness.

> We lie down in our shame and our reproach covers us for we have sinned against the Lord our God . . . and have not obeyed the voice of our God.
> —JEREMIAH 3:25

> My people are destroyed for lack of knowledge . . . The more they increased the more they sinned against Me, I will change their glory into shame.
> —HOSEA 4:6–7

The effects of the shame of our sins can be devastating, depressing, paralyzing and crippling. Like a vessel overcome by the power of the sea or shipwrecked on jagged rocks along forbidden paths, our souls seem doomed to languish and perish as they mourn their demise.

What can we do to heal from the daily onslaughts of man's

shame and ensure that we do not become prey to its devices? What can we do to keep from inflicting the same pain on others and from being tempted to engage in its venomous tactics? What can we do to disentangle ourselves from the deadly web of shame that has been inflicted upon us? We can call upon the name of Jesus. It is Jesus, the living Word, who can save us and heal us. It is He who bore the reproach and shame of our sins on the cross. He humbled Himself and hung in shame on the cross for the whole world to see. He was shamed before His family and friends. This He did for you and me. "Jesus . . . who for the joy that was set before Him endured the cross, despising the shame, and has sat down at the right hand of the throne of God" (Hebrews 12:2). His shame on the cross paid the price for our deliverance, restoration and honor. When we are ashamed, He knows how it feels and is ever willing and able to heal us. When we stoop to shaming others, He understands, because he bore our sin and is ever willing to forgive. By His blood He washed our shame away, by His resurrection power He enables us to extinguish shame and live to honor Him. By His stripes we are healed of the devastating effects of shaming and of being shamed. Whether or not our sinful actions and thoughts are self-motivated or induced as a reaction to outside onslaughts, pressures or temptations, we need to come to Jesus who bore our shame on the cross. We need to allow Him to make us whole. In His blood there is power and provision for our healing.

> And I will establish My covenant with you. Then shall you know that I am the Lord, that you may remember and be ashamed, and never open your mouth anymore because of your shame, when I provide you an atonement for all you have done, says the Lord God.
> —EZEKIEL 16:62–63

In His mercy for us, Christ died for us and washed us clean

with His own blood. In His mercy and compassion, He empowers us with His resurrection power to transform our hearts and minds from vessels of shame to vessels filled with His glory and honor. For His name's sake, He paid the price for our deliverance with his own blood, that we wouldn't perish in our shame but continue our voyage in fulfillment of His Word. Let us repent and accept this great gift and continue our voyage to eternal glory.

> I counsel you to buy from Me gold refined in the fire, that you may be rich, and white garments, that you may be clothed, that the shame of your nakedness may not be revealed; and anoint your eyes with salve, that you may see . . . .Therefore be zealous and repent.
> —REVELATION 3:18-19

Let us repent and allow God to clothe us with His righteousness and honor. Let us allow Him to empower us to turn our eyes from darkness and our hurts, sin and shame to behold Him who is full of majesty, honor and glory.

FROM SHAME TO VICTORY

FOR MANY YEARS I didn't understand the paralyzing sting of shame—not until I was dealing with self-inflicted guilt, as well as situations of abandonment, abuse and slander that spread like wildfire. It was like being pulled to the bottom of the sea. But the hand of the Lord gently guided me up and taught me by His Word to, once again, find the harbor of His presence. Like a lighthouse secure on a rock, He is forever there to lead us to the victory in store for us.

> Do not rejoice over me, my enemy; when I fall, I will arise; when I sit in darkness, the Lord will be a light to me . . . He will bring me forth to the light.
> —MICAH 7:8-9

The Lord is my light and my salvation... Your word is a lamp unto my feet and a light to my path.

—PSALM 27:1; 119:105

... that you may proclaim the praises of Him who called you out of darkness into his marvelous light.

—1 PETER 2:9

FROM SHAME TO HONOR

WHEN WE ARE in darkness, we are surrounded by pain and shame. But in His presence there is joy and comfort; strength and beauty and honor and light. When we walk in His light, we walk in His honor and love.

Honor and majesty are before Him; Strength and gladness are in His place.

—1 CHRONICLES 16:27

Strength and beauty are in His sanctuary.

—PSALM 96:6

By humility and the fear of the Lord are riches and honor and life.

—PROVERBS 22:4

If anyone serves Me, him My Father will honor.

—JOHN 12:26

You are clothed with honor and majesty...
Who cover Yourself with light as with a garment.

—PSALM 104:1-2

FROM SHAME TO HONOR IN THE FAMILY

IN A SMALL SURVEY asking parents how they can bring honor to their own family, the following answers were given: by obeying God, by honoring God, by forgiving, by loving the family, by providing and protecting, by teaching and obeying the

Word of God, by expecting godliness, by respecting one another, by humbly serving one another, by a husband loving his wife as Christ loved the Church. When Christ obeyed the Father by bearing the shame of our sins on the cross, He honored the Father and brought honor to the whole family of God and to the Body of Christ, His bride. In so doing, He became the ultimate example for husbands to honor their wives and for sons and daughters to honor their parents.

It is possible for parents to bring honor or shame to their children, or for children to bring honor or shame to their parents. We are to honor one another.

> He who mistreats his father and chases away his mother
> Is a son who causes shame and brings reproach.
> —PROVERBS 19:26

> A wise son makes a father glad,
> But a foolish man despises his mother.
> —PROVERBS 15:20

> Honor you father and your mother.
> —MARK 7:10

> Let love be without hypocrisy . . . be kindly affectionate to one another with brotherly love, in honor giving preference to one another.
> —ROMANS 12:9–10

SHAME AND HONOR IN A NATION

INDEED, WHAT BRINGS honor to God and to a family also brings honor to a whole nation. In contrast, what dishonors God and a family also dishonors a people. This is a day when America is turning more and more away from God's laws, power and provision. We, as a nation, as well as individuals, are in grave danger of experiencing a severe decline in morale, self-esteem, honor and strength. What will it take for us, as individuals and as a nation, to turn from our sin and shame to Jesus, the author and finisher of our faith? Only when we turn back to God and honor Him by our obedience to Him will He honor and bless us.

> Righteousness exalts a nation,
> But sin is a reproach to any people.
>
> —PROVERBS 14:34

> Blessed is the nation whose God is the Lord.
>
> —PSALM 33:12

Unfortunately, even in America, a nation founded "under God," the last decade of the 20th century was characterized by the dismantling of traditional values, and by increasingly penalizing and shaming the "moral majority." However, widespread decadence is treated with approval and even applause.

> But the unjust knows no shame.
>
> —ZEPHANIAH 3:5

We need to repent as a nation and come back to God, who has blessed us so abundantly. What will it take to find our way back to the Judeo-Christian values on which this country was founded so that we may continue our journey through history in honor of our Creator? What will it take for nations around the world to repent and become a living testimony to God's honor and glory?

> ... the great city, the holy Jerusalem, descending out of heaven from God ... for the glory of God illuminated it ... And the nations of those who are saved shall walk in its light, and the kings of the earth bring their glory and honor into it.
>
> —REVELATION 21:10, 23, 24

Let us pray that our nation will humble itself and return to God, to walk in His glory and honor. Let us stand firm in the changing winds and waves, upholding God's truths and standards. Let us take heart and encourage one another to stand fast in the hour of adversity. Let us encourage each other to follow the sights and sounds of the heavenly lighthouse, our Lord Jesus Christ, who leads us safely to the Father and the harbor of His love, peace and protection.

Any person or family can bring honor or dishonor to a whole community. Figures of authority, like kings or presidents, can bring honor or shame to a whole nation, as we have seen throughout the history of the world. Any person or nation walking in sin and shame dishonors the name of the Lord. But God is worthy and desirous of His name's honor and praise.

> But a wicked man is loathsome and comes to shame.
> —PROVERBS 13:5

> When the wicked comes, contempt comes also;
> And with dishonor comes reproach.
> —PROVERBS 18:3

> ...they defiled it by their own ways and deeds... wherever they went they profaned My holy name...but for My holy name's sake... I will sanctify My great name,... and the nations shall know that I am the Lord, says the Lord God...I will cleanse you from all your filthiness...I will give you a new heart...I will put My Spirit within you and cause you to walk in My statutes.
> —EZEKIEL 36:17, 20-27

FROM SHAME TO DELIVERANCE

SOME WAYS OF causing shame and dishonor are: slandering, stealing, betraying, humiliating, manipulating, hating, abusing, mocking, abandoning, persecuting, neglecting, harming, mutilating and killing. These can occur in the realm of the conscience, the body, the emotions, the intellect or the spirit. Individuals, families, communities or whole nations can fall victim to or perpetrate them.

Some ways to produce honor are: loving, caring, encouraging, praising, thanking, providing, protecting, forgiving, forbearing, obeying and informing.

Some of the roots of shame are: unbelief, rebellion, hopelessness, hatred, lying, guilt, envy, covetousness, lust, unfaithfulness and defiance. Conversely, some of the roots of honor are: faith, hope, love, obedience, loyalty, purity, honesty and patience.

> All who forsake You shall be ashamed.
> —JEREMIAH 17:13

> Behold, I lay in Zion a stumbling stone and rock of offense. And whoever believes on Him will not be put to shame.
> —ROMANS 9:33

> But Israel shall be saved by the Lord with an everlasting salvation; you shall not be ashamed or disgraced forever.
> —ISAIAH 45:17

> Because He has set his love upon me, therefore will I deliver him; I will set him on high; because he has known My name. He shall call upon Me and I will answer him, I will be with him in trouble; I will deliver him, and honor him.
> —PSALM 91:14-15

How privileged we are that God, who sits on His throne in majesty and power, reaches down to deliver us from perishing in our sin and shame and sets our feet on higher ground. He clothes us with His own garments of peace, honor and glory—to the honor and glory of His name.

> But glory, honor and peace to everyone who works what is good, to the Jew first and also to the Greek.
> —ROMANS 2:10

> What is man that You are mindful of him? And the son of man that You visit him? For You have made him a little

lower than the angels, and you have crowned him with glory and honor.

—HEBREWS 2:6–7

Let us allow God to deliver and heal us. Let us come into His presence. Let us allow His love to transform our shipwrecked hearts from despair and shame to hope and honor. Let us be vessels of deliverance for His glory in everyday living, and continue our voyage in His name and in His power.

FROM SHAME TO DIGNITY

IN THE PROCESS of our journey from shame to glory, we can be instruments of deliverance for other shipwrecked hearts. Sometimes it takes only a smile, a kind word or a helping hand to lift someone from a bout of despair and shame to a haven of honor, dignity and hope. One kind word can mean the difference between night and day, life and death. Wherever Jesus went, He wrought miracles of healing and deliverance. He brought life, dignity, comfort and honor to individuals. He came to save and to serve mankind. Likewise, we are to serve and honor one another:

> Be kindly affectionate to one another with brotherly love in honor giving preference to one another.
>
> —ROMANS 12:10

Believers in Christ Jesus, as part of His Body, are responsible to fulfill this command in our everyday lives. We must do this in order to heal as individuals, as families, as church families, as communities and as a nation. Very young children perceive the difference between honor and shame. God-fearing children that have been honored and loved won't have any difficulty honoring their elders. We learn to love one another at a very young age by Christ's example, by the Holy Spirit and by God-abiding people in our lives. As we heal and mature, we have

113

VOYAGE—THE JOURNEY TO ETERNAL GLORY

the great privilege of becoming God's vessels of love and honor. We are instruments of restoration for the Body of Christ, as well as for unbelievers.

One of my Christian friends in California had suffered in her teenage years from the embarrassment of limping. One leg was two inches shorter than the other. As a young lady, she found this humiliating factor in her life often insurmountable. Even during her marriage, she found herself, at times, humiliated by her back-slidden husband. Being very distressed one day, she visited me and talked non-stop for a great length of time. I silently prayed, and soon God prompted me to look her straight in the eyes and pronounce, "Jesus!" She stopped talking abruptly. We proceeded to ponder upon, discuss and revel in the power of the name of Jesus. Suddenly she began to laugh and cry. She praised the Lord and danced around. She exclaimed, "Look what happened! I'm not limping! I've never been able to stand straight up, let alone jump or run with such ease!" She walked home that day with a miracle in her body and new dignity and love in her heart.

Whether we feel ashamed by a body crippled by war or disease or by a heart and mind maimed by abuse, guilt or abandonment, God is eager to restore us into the image of His beloved Son, Christ Jesus. Shame can be inflicted by ourselves, family members or society as a whole. However, God can use us, our families, our church and our community to restore dignity and honor, and make us whole.

FROM SHAME TO WISDOM

ANOTHER ROOT OF honor is the fear of the Lord. When we walk in the fear of the Lord, we produce wisdom and honor. On the contrary, when the fear of the Lord is absent we produce foolishness and shame.

The fear of the Lord is the beginning of knowledge.
But fools despise wisdom and instruction.

—PROVERBS 1:7

By humility and the fear of the Lord
Are riches and honor and life.

—PROVERBS 22:4

The wise shall inherit glory,
But shame shall be the legacy of fools.

—PROVERBS 3:35

Wisdom is the principal thing . . .
Exalt her, and she will promote you;
She will bring you honor, when you embrace her . . .
A crown of glory she will deliver to you.

—PROVERBS 4: 7-9

When we walk in the fear of the Lord, we walk in honor and wisdom. As Christians, we need to be delivered from every trace of foolishness and shame. We need to flee temptations that so easily beset us in everyday life. We need to run from sin and the ensuing shame that can linger in our hearts. We continually need to be cleansed and restored to bring honor to His name. Let us be vessels of restoration and instruments of peace, honor and healing to others who suffer from shame. Let us, as individuals, families and communities be wise and fight a good fight, running the race to reach our destiny ordained by His grace—the glorious harbor of His presence.

> . . . let us lay aside every weight, and the sin which so easily ensnares us, and let us run with endurance the race that is set before us, looking unto Jesus, author and finisher of our faith.
>
> —HEBREWS 12:1

And let us consider one another in order to stir up love and good works.

—HEBREWS 10:24

FROM SHAME TO THE CROSS

ANOTHER TYPE OF shame is incurred by the persecution that arises at times towards Christians. Since the time of Christ, believers around the world have endured tremendous tribulations and shame. They have been slandered, shunned, accused, abused, tortured and killed. Those are experiences that bring the love, faith and obedience of the child of God to the maximum test. Those encounters with worldly forces ultimately reveal to us and to the world the intensity of His love and the power of enduring in Him. They are also an opportunity to identify with the shame and sufferings of Christ—an opportunity to take up one's cross to follow Him. But at the end of the race, those who have followed the course of the cross in the light of his Word shall share in His triumph and glory of His kingdom.

> If you are reproached for the name of Christ, blessed are you for the Spirit of glory and of God rests upon you.
> —1 PETER 4:14

> Therefore I take pleasure in infirmities, in reproaches, in needs, in persecutions, in distresses, for Christ's sake. For when I am weak, then I am strong.
> —2 CORINTHIANS 12:10

> But in all things approving ourselves as ministers of God: in much patience, in tribulations . . . by the word of truth, by the power of God, by the armor of righteousness . . . by honor and dishonor.
> —2 CORINTHIANS 6:4, 7-8

When we suffer shame due to persecution for Christ's sake, our shame turns to joy deepened and intensified like gold refined in fire. Early Christians, as well as many believers around the world have experienced this on a regular basis and often in unexpected circumstances.

So they departed from the presence of the council, rejoicing that they were counted worthy to suffer shame for His name.

—ACTS 5:41

FROM SHAME TO REPENTANCE

THERE IS ANOTHER type of shame that has a godly purpose. It is the shame that leads our hearts to repentance and to the forgiving power of our Savior. It is remorse for having dishonored God and ourselves by our own sin. This shame is the catalyst to hunger for God and for a restored relationship with Him. We need it on a daily basis to become whole and walk uprightly in His sight. We desperately need it as a nation today, lest we become more and more like Sodom and Gomorrah and allow sin to become the accepted norm in our society. Oh, that God would renew our conscience and grant our nation a new sense of wholesome shame and remorse. Let us yearn for a fresh hunger for God and His righteousness.

GODLY SHAME

THERE IS ANOTHER type of shame that is born in the purposes of God—the shame of godly foolishness. Throughout history, mankind has achieved tremendous feats in his own wisdom, only to find out in the end that, despite all his knowledge and worldly wisdom, man's heart hasn't changed. It is still heading towards personal death and global pollution and destruction. Can the world save and heal itself? Indeed, according to God's Word, it cannot, lest any man should boast. Man's wisdom is foolishness in the sight of God. And God has a plan for salvation that seems foolish in the sight of man.

Are we willing to become godly fools in order to become truly wise? Are we willing to trade our own intellect for godly wisdom that leads to life eternal? Are we willing to be fools for Christ and proclaim the good news of the redemptive power of

His blood? Can we humble ourselves to appropriate God's wisdom, which is foolishness in the sight of the world? Are we humble enough to be fools in order to spread the good news of salvation? Are we willing to be fools in the world to become lighthouses, pouring forth the light that is in Christ Jesus? Is our compassion deep enough to endure ridicule in order to rescue the lost who are sinking in the sea of sin and searching for the harbor of eternal life.

> For the wisdom of the world is foolishness with God.
> —1 CORINTHIANS 3:19

> Because the foolishness of God is wiser than men, and the weakness of God is stronger than man...But God has chosen the foolish things of the world to put to shame the wise... that no flesh should glory in His presence...For since, in the wisdom of God, the world through wisdom did not know God, it pleased God through the foolishness of the message preached to save those who believe. But the natural man does not receive the things of the Spirit of God, for they are foolishness to him; for the message of the cross is foolishness to those who are perishing, but to us who are being saved it is the power of God.
> —1 CORINTHIANS 1:25, 27, 29, 21; 2:14; 1:18

> We are fools for Christ's sake, but you are wise in Christ.
> —1 CORINTHIANS 4:10

> ...for we have made a spectacle to the world...being reviled, we bless; being persecuted, we endure; being defamed, we entreat.
> —1 CORINTHIANS 4:9, 12–13

SHAME OF PRIDE

SOME OF THE shame that we experience is the shame that is preceded by our pride. We need to repent of all of our pride in

118

its many forms. It is pride that results from self-sufficiency, self-exaltation, greed, power, control and accomplishments. It is the pride that exalts itself above the knowledge of God and goes beyond the healthy sense of self-esteem that is produced by trusting in God. It is a pride that is a form of idolatry and a cause for God's chastisement.

> Do not be wise in your own eyes.
> —PROVERBS 3:7

> Pride goes before destruction,
> And a haughty spirit before a fall.
> —PROVERBS 16:18

> I will halt the arrogance of the proud, and I will lay low the haughtiness of the terrible.
> —ISAIAH 13:11

> Woe to the crown of pride . . . whose glorious beauty is a fading flower.
> —ISAIAH 28:1

> Though you ascend as high as the eagle, and though you set your nest among the stars, from there I will bring you down, says the Lord.
> —OBADIAH 1:4

In a culture in which self-sufficiency, selfishness and self-exaltation are encouraged on a daily basis, it is difficult for Christians to walk obediently and humbly before the Lord. We are admonished to cast down the high and lofty things of man and to refrain from taking on man's weapons, rather than God's weapons, in the everyday battles of life.

> For though we walk in the flesh, we do not war after the flesh: For the weapons of our warfare are not carnal, but mighty through God to the pulling down of strongholds; casting down imaginations, and every high thing that

119

exalts itself against the knowledge of God, and bringing into captivity every thought to the obedience of Christ.
—2 CORINTHIANS 10:3–5

FROM SHAME TO HUMILITY AND FAVOR

THERE IS A great difference between humility and humiliation. It is important to realize that when God seeks to bring down the proud and self-exalted, His intention and final goal is to tear down the idolatry that pride engages in. "I am the Lord, that is My name, and My glory I will not give to another" (Isaiah 42:8). This process can be humiliating to the rebellious heart, but to those who welcome the discipline of the Lord, it is a process towards repentance, healing and humility. God's discipline for the repenting believer then becomes a tool to create a Christ-like character and demeanor. The renewed believer then walks in humility with Him who walked humbly among mankind. When we humble ourselves, God Himself shows His favor to us:

The Lord raises those who are bowed down.
—PSALM 146:8

And whosoever exalts himself will be humbled, and he who humbles himself will be exalted.
—MATTHEW 23:12

They walk, O Lord, in the light of Your countenance . . .
And in your righteousness they are exalted.
For You are the glory of their strength
And in Your favor our horn is exalted.
—PSALM 89:15–17

The fear of the Lord is the instruction of wisdom,
And before honor is humility.
—PROVERBS 15:33

Let this mind be in you which was also in Christ Jesus, . . .

He humbled Himself and became obedient to the point of
death, even the death of the cross.

—PHILIPPIANS 2:5, 8

FROM SHAME TO LOVE

IT IS, HOWEVER, vital to remember that, in our quest for humility,
we need to humble ourselves in a wholesome manner and to
edify one another, especially those in the Body of Christ. Those
who are guilt-ridden and deeply ashamed due to a lack of repentance, or who have experienced humiliating abuse may have a
tendency towards self-abasement or self-abuse. It is sometimes a
difficult process to reverse this tendency. But in the light of
God's Word, by the power of the Holy Spirit and with the love of
God's people, we can all learn to honor and love oneself in a
wholesome manner. Jesus admonished, "You shall love your
neighbor as yourself" (Matt. 19:19). We are also admonished by
the Apostle Paul to walk in love and meekness:" ... put on tender
mercies, kindness, humility, meekness, longsuffering; ... But
above all these things put on love ... " (Col. 3:12, 14).

How can we learn to love ourselves when there is a lack of
love within us and around us? In the book of Jude we are
encouraged to walk in the love of God, and by the words of
Jesus we are called to learn from Him:

> But you, beloved, building yourselves up on your most
> holy faith, praying in the Holy Spirit, keep yourselves in
> the love of God, looking for the mercy of our Lord Jesus
> Christ unto eternal life.
>
> —JUDE 1:20, 21

> Take My yoke upon you and learn from Me, for I am gentle
> and lowly in heart, and you will find rest for your soul.
>
> —MATTHEW 11:29

We are to pray and learn from Jesus, Himself, how to walk in
humility and in love. We need to take His yoke upon us, to let

His love, humility and grace cover the shame inflicted upon us by others and by ourselves. Let us learn to love from Him who knows the Father and His love. Let us learn to love by knowing the One who loved us first and whose sacrificial love made provision for overcoming our shame.

> Nor does anyone know the Father except the Son, and the one to whom the Son wills to reveal Him.
> —MATTHEW 11:27

> Now by this we know that we know Him, if we keep His commandments. But whoever keeps His word, truly the love of God is perfected in Him.
> —1 JOHN 1:3, 5

> ...and everyone who loves is born of God and knows God.
> —1 JOHN 4:7

> For whatever is born of God overcomes the world.
> —1 JOHN 5:4

Let us be overcomers of the things of the world outside and within us. Let us heal and overcome the effects of shame by learning to love ourselves as Christ has loved us. Let us honor Him by learning to walk in His love and honor. Let us allow Him who conquered the sting and shame of death to exercise His victory within us.

> Death is swallowed up in victory. But thanks be to God, who gives us the victory through our Lord Jesus Christ.
> —1 CORINTHIANS 15:54, 57

In order for us to overcome our shame and to truly love one another as we love ourselves, we need to appropriate Christ's victory. In humility we need to accept God's provision to overcome and to surrender our own attempts to cover our shame. After Adam and Eve sinned, they experienced shame and fear and a need to cover themselves, and to hide from the presence of the Lord. But their covering was insufficient and unacceptable in the sight of God. He then provided them with a covering. How often we attempt to cover our shame by our own devices. Whether it be materialism, fame, addictions, overachievement, false religions or any of a myriad of other ways to compensate for deep-rooted shame, it will only bring about devastation. Only God's holy love, made available to us by Christ's redemptive death on the cross, can properly cleanse, heal and deliver. As we journey through life, let us not allow our vessels to be capsized by our shame. Instead, let us be fully restored in the presence of His love—not in our own wisdom and strength but in the power and wisdom of God. His glory and honor shall be forevermore.

One Christmas, I was traveling by plane to visit my sister in Atlanta and to celebrate the joy of the season with her. During the flight, I gazed out the window and observed "ceilings" of clouds passing by. I watched as the magnificent sea of clouds gave birth to different formations. First, they resembled an enormous herd of sheep, then numerous wings of angels. At one point, there was an open space through which I could detect, 30,000 feet below, a river in the shape of an "S" reflecting the sun's rays like burning gold. It seemed to exclaim, "Glory be to our glorious Savior."

Within minutes, other formations appeared like mountains of wool and like castles in the sky. Then, in the top layer, a whisper of clouds floated by, as though on the soft breeze of the breath of the Lord. There came a hush in the air as shadows of dusk were slowly approaching. Gradually, the clouds seemed to awaken and come alive as they increasingly reflected the brilliant rays of a setting sun. They seemed to shout, "Glory be to the Lord who giveth light and who is our light."

Eventually, formations of a strong hand emerged embracing another hand. It inspired me to pray. As I prayed and meditated, the Lord said to me, "With My strong hand will I feed you; with My love I will affirm you." What an encouraging word that was for me. I thought of the beauty and strength we gain as His love is reflected in our hearts. I thought of the honor and glory of His name and how we honor Him and are honored by allowing His light to shine in our hearts. In His light the shadows of sin, shame and death disperse. In His light, we are awakened to a glorious new beginning of significance, beauty, strength, healing and love. Christ wasn't born among us to condemn us or to leave us in our shame. He was born to die in shame on our behalf and to clothe us with His robe of righteousness, honor and glory.

It is crucial for us to receive this free gift of salvation. It is also crucial for us to open our hearts' doors to receive and to honor the King of Glory. Let us be like the wise men who came from afar to honor and worship Him and to offer Him their costly gifts. Let us offer Him our hearts and acknowledge Him as Redeemer and King of our lives. Let us lay aside the tendencies to rule over our own lives, failures, thoughts and emotions in our own strength. Let us forsake idolatry and rebellion that will inevitably disgrace and destroy the rulership of Christ within us. How often our actions betray us and demonstrate attitudes that seek to shame and to destroy the Kingship of Christ within us. King Herod exhibited the idolatry of his heart by killing a multitude of Israel's infant sons. We might not follow his cruel example, but how often, I wonder, have we indulged in a type of idolatry that shames and crucifies Christ in our hearts and in one another?

Since the tender moments of childhood, Christ was persecuted and sought to be killed. For over thirty years, no one was able to kill Him. At the right time, He, who could have called upon armies of angels, willingly laid down His life for us and allowed Himself to be crucified as a ransom for our sins. Let us not persecute, but welcome, worship and embrace the

Christ who was born in a manger to be King and Savior in our hearts. Let us bear His name in His honor. Let us honor Him and let Him be King.

Several days before Christmas, my sister Greti had opened her home to international students from around the world. She and her husband had done this for many years. What an opportunity it was to explain the gospel message by way of the true meaning of Christmas. Many students shared various stories about Christmas traditions around the world and the impact Christ had made in their lives. Christ's birth was celebrated in songs of several different languages.

On Christmas eve, at the candlelight service of the Church I used to attend, Pastor Ron Crews spoke eloquently of God's desire to embrace us with His redeeming love. God the Father tenderly demonstrated this desire in His Son's birth. His Son was born to lay down His life for us. This demonstration of God's love has set precedent on how we are to love and embrace one another in His name. After the lighting of candles and the partaking of holy communion, the congregation was encouraged to express God's love to one another. As people's faces lit up in the love of Christ, the King of glory was made manifest and honored. He was welcomed to be our Redeemer and King that Christmas eve. He was worshiped in song and honored with the greatest gift we can give to Him— our love for Him and for one another.

FROM SHAME TO SACRIFICIAL LOVE

IN ORDER TO save us from our sin, Christ sacrificially paid our penalty by dying in our stead. The blood that He shed on Calvary was the ultimate expression of His and the Father's love for mankind. It took Christ's sacrifice for mankind to be restored from despair to hope, from death to life, from darkness to light and from shame to dignity and honor.

Even though throughout history there have been men, women and children who have sacrificially laid down their lives for their faith in Christ or for another human being, our everyday lives do not usually warrant such dramatic acts of sacrifice. However, we can provide numerous kinds of sacrificial expressions of love and honor to the Lord and to one another in our daily lives. Every day there are opportunities around us to be an example and an expression of Christ's character of sacrificial love.

I remember the day my mother walked several miles in the scorching heat to buy a used bicycle for me. I remember when she took a chocolate bar that had been donated to us, and gave it to a poor gypsy girl. Even though I had often been hungry myself and had never had a whole chocolate bar before, I considered it an honor to bring a token of joy to someone more needy than I. I remember my sister walking a mile in knee-high snow with me to help me find a dying friend. I remember a father sleeplessly guarding the fireplace all night to keep the family warm and safe during a winter storm.

How costly it was for our Heavenly Father to ensure redemption for mankind. How costly it was for His Son to pay the ransom for our sin. What price are we willing to pay to offer tokens of sacrificial love and honor? When Christ was born, the wise men brought Him costly gifts befitting a new-born King. Before Christ's death, Mary anointed Him with a most costly oil befitting the King who was about to sacrifice His life for His people. What sacrifices of love and honor shall we bring to the King of Kings? What sacrifices shall we give to one another?

FROM SHAME TO TRUST AND INTIMACY

THERE ARE SOME aspects of honor and shame that can also affect our health, our character, our state of mind and our relationships. Some of the painful effects of shame include fear, depression, anxiety, bitterness, illness, idleness, eating disorders, hostility, insomnia, addictions, violence, hopelessness, apathy and loneliness. Some of the aspects of honor, on the other hand, are happiness, health, love, joy, peace, enthusiasm, caring, gentleness, friendship and intimacy.

> Let not mercy and truth forsake you . . . find favor and high esteem in the sight of God and man.
>
> . . . Fear the Lord and depart from evil.
> It will be health to your flesh, and strength to your bones.
>
> My son, do not forget my law.
> But let your heart keep my commandments,
> For length of days and long life
> And peace they will add to you.
> —PROVERBS 3:3-4, 7-8, 1-2

As we honor God, in obedience to Him, He honors us and provides for us. The character and strength in any relationship depends greatly upon love and honor. Closeness, trust and intimacy in a relationship also thrive on love and honor. It is important to honor and be honored personally as well as publicly. Even God the Father publicly honored His Son saying, "This is My beloved Son in whom I am well pleased" (Matt. 3:17). Likewise, Jesus publicly honored the woman who honored Him by sacrificially anointing Him with very costly oil.

> A woman came to Him having an alabaster flask of very costly fragrant oil, and she poured it on His head . . . Jesus . . . said to them . . . wherever this gospel is preached in the whole world, what this woman has done will also be told as a memorial to her.
> —MATTHEW 26:7, 10, 13

Are we, the body and Bride of Christ, honoring Him by sacrificially offering our oil of gladness, praise and thanksgiving for what He has done for us on the cross? Are we offering our highest praise to the One who will acknowledge us before the Father?

> He who overcomes shall be clothed in white garments, and I will not blot out His name from the Book of Life, but I will confess his name before My Father and before His angels.
>
> —REVELATION 3:5

Shame causes distance in a relationship between God and man. It also causes distance between individuals and among families, communities and nations. But honor nourishes relationships and causes them to flourish and become bulwarks of strength.

> But a woman who fears the Lord, she shall be praised.
>
> The heart of her husband safely trusts her;
> . . . She does him good and not evil
> All the days of her life.
>
> Strength and honor are her clothing; she opens her
>   mouth with wisdom,
> And on her tongue is the law of kindness.
>
> . . . Yes, she reaches out her hands to the needy.
>
> She watches over the ways of her household . . .
> Her children rise up and call her blessed;
> Her husband also, and he praises her.
>
> —PROVERBS 31:30, 11-12, 25-26, 20, 27-28

The same principle, as in this example of a virtuous woman, applies to the Church—the Bride of Christ. The more we honor Him, the more we are honored and the closer and more intimate a relationship we have with Him on a daily basis. The reverse is true as well. The closer we draw near to God, the more we honor Him and are honored and blessed by Him.

For indeed, those who are far from you shall perish . . .
But it is good for me to draw near to God;
I have put my trust in the Lord God,
That I may declare all Your works.

—PSALM 73:27-28

Come near to Me, hear this . . . Thus says the Lord, your
Redeemer, the Holy One of Israel; I am the Lord your God,
who teaches you to profit, who leads you by the way you
should go. Oh, that you had heeded My commandments!
Then your peace would have been like a river, and your
righteousness like the waves of the sea.

—ISAIAH 48:16-18

Indeed it was Jesus, our Heavenly Bridegroom, who shed
His own blood for us, His Bride, that we may approach and
come near the Father. He made the way for us to boldly enter
His presence.

Therefore, brethren, having boldness to enter the Holiest by
the blood of Jesus . . . let us draw near with a true heart in
full assurance of faith, having our hearts sprinkled from an
evil conscience and our bodies washed with pure water.

—HEBREWS 10:19, 22

Coming near to God also requires a certain amount of trust.
The more we appropriate His Word—that He indeed is a righteous God and fully trustworthy—and the more we heed His
call to trust in Him, the closer our relationship will be with Him.

During my years of teaching in Christian schools, from levels
of kindergarten through college, I observed that many students
who did not have a trusting relationship with God or their parents, often fell into mischief and, in turn, couldn't be trusted. In
all the times I didn't fully trust God, I felt I couldn't trust myself
and my actions. My actions seemed directly affected by my relationship with God and God's people.

Our ability to trust in God is greatly affected by our knowledge of His Word and our willingness to appropriate it into our daily lives. The greatest enemies of a trusting relationship with God are ignorance, fear, rebellion, pride and self-sufficiency. Both our sin and our reactions to injuries inflicted on us can hinder us from trusting in God and coming to Him for renewal, comfort, deliverance, restoration and healing. Our lack of trust in Him further contributes to a perpetual cycle of sin, idolatry and hurt. And that creates an even greater distance between us and hinders a vital relationship with our Heavenly Father.

Oh, that we may learn to trust in God. Oh, that our hearts may yearn to know Him who is trustworthy beyond measure. Let us embark on and continue our journey upon the sea of His faithfulness, power and strength. Let us ride upon the cleansing, refreshing waters of His Word in order to bring into His harbor the harvest of the sea of grace. Let us bring to Him the good fruit produced by our trust in Him—in honor of His name.

> In you, O Lord, I put my trust;
> Let me never be ashamed.
>
> —PSALM 31:1

> ... that we should not trust in ourselves but in God who raises the dead.
>
> —2 CORINTHIANS 1:9

> Trust in Him at all times, you people.
>
> —PSALM 62:8

When God sent His only begotten Son to live among us, to minister, to be tempted and finally to die on the cross for our sins, He exercised utmost trust in Him. Likewise, Jesus, who has perfect knowledge of the Father, exercised total trust in Him when He hung on the cross and committed His imminent death into God's hands. "Father, into Your hands I commit My spirit" (Luke 23:46).

Some types of shame can hinder a trusting, close relationship with God and can be caused by circumstances or environment. Examples of these are: war, illness, grief, social injustice, natural disasters, shattered dreams, handicaps, separation from loved ones, childlessness, famine, poverty, divorce and death in the family, the community or the nation. In all these afflictions, God can reach down and meet us in the innermost chambers of our hearts. There is no place or circumstance that will hinder God from revealing Himself to those who cry out for His comfort and deliverance.

> In you, O Lord, I put my trust;
> Let me never be ashamed;
> Deliver me in Your righteousness.
> For You are my rock and my fortress.
> . . . You are my strength.
> . . . You have redeemed me, O Lord God of truth.
>
> I will extol You, O Lord, for You have lifted me up . . .
> O Lord my God, I cried out to You,
> And You healed me. O Lord, You brought my soul up
>   from the grave;
> You have kept me alive.
>   —PSALM 31:1, 3, 4-5; 30:1-2
>
> For in the time of trouble . . .
> He shall set me high upon a rock.
> And now my head shall be lifted up above my enemies
>   all around me . . .
> When you said "Seek My face" my heart said to You,
>   "Your face Lord, I will seek."
>   —PSALM 27: 5-6, 8

FROM SHAME TO THE LIGHT ON THE ROCK

IN THE COURSE of our lives, our circumstances and the condition of our hearts and minds take on many shapes. They change according to our needs, purpose and direction. As we travel through life's journey, we become various types of vessels of

God's grace. Our struggles, goals and purposes resemble different kinds of ships at sea. Some are pleasure boats, frolicking in the winds and waves or resting safely in the harbor. Others are fishing boats—small or great—created to gather the harvest of the sea. Then there are icebreakers, slicing a path through ice and snow. There are explorers' ships; in the olden days they were rudimentary but firm, and in modern days they are equipped with instruments to explore the treasures of the sea. There are lifeboats to save lives from peril, and tugboats that guide gigantic ships to the harbor. Finally, there are submarines and battleships ever ready to conquer and defend.

Are we trained and equipped with all of God's artillery to conquer and to defend, in His honor, the borders of the kingdom of heaven within us? Are we committed to claiming within us, at all costs, the land of freedom in Christ Jesus that is ordained for us to possess by grace? Are we willing to cross the deep waters of our lives, in high tides and low tides, in storms or sunny days to run the race to reach His glorious presence?

> . . . and let us run with endurance the race that is set before us, looking unto Jesus.
> —HEBREWS 12:1-2

> I press toward the goal for the prize of the upward call of God in Christ Jesus.
> —PHILIPPIANS 3:14

Let us press on to traverse the sea of defeat, death and shame to reach the shores of His glorious kingdom. Let us allow His Word to be an anchor in the storm, a lighthouse firmly planted on the rock and a fire in the engine of our vessels. Let us obediently adjust to the winds of the Holy Spirit. Let us allow Jesus to be captain of our hearts, minds and souls, so that we may enter into the harbor of the Father's presence. Let us victoriously finish the race and, in His honor, triumphantly complete our journey ordained by grace.

CHAPTER 17

MEETING GOD
IN THE WILDERNESS

THROUGHOUT LIFE'S JOURNEY, God provides harbors of rest and restoration in order to enable us to continue our voyage empowered by His grace. Occasionally, we seek refuge in the wilderness to draw strength and new inspiration. However, sometimes we seem to travel off course and unintentionally get stranded in a desert before reaching our final destination, God's kingdom and presence. Other times, we get tempted by the sight of a lush island and, against our better judgment, we wander too close to it, unable to sail away. As time goes on, we realize the futility of our mistake and, in spite of all its lushness, the island seems to turn into a desert and a prison.

Whenever we find ourselves lost in nature's deserts, we seem to walk a fine line between life and death. It may be similarly alarming to find ourselves in a state of inward wilderness. It is a desert of the heart, mind and soul. How do we survive in the wilderness? How do we find our way out? How can anyone benefit from and find purpose in a wilderness experience? Let us allow history and God's Word to show the way.

Throughout the ages the wilderness and deserts have been not only places of misdirection and exile but also places of refuge, purpose and retreat. For certain individuals and groups of people they have become some of the most significant locations on earth. They have been places of profound encounters between God and man that changed the course of nations.

Jesus went to the wilderness to pray, to retreat and to fulfill a specific task. It was there that he proved His utmost purity by resisting all of Satan's temptations. It was there that He established once and for all His divine character as the spotless Lamb of God. He established His eligibility to be Mediator between us and God. He resisted every temptation by way of the written Word. Finally, He, who was the Word made flesh, commanded Satan to depart. Jesus then emerged from the desert to fulfill His mission for the deliverance of all mankind—to shed His blood for the forgiveness of our sins. He emerged from the desert as the great Shepherd who would lay down His life for His sheep.

When Moses went to the wilderness of Mt. Horeb, he went there to herd sheep. It was there that God called him, by way of an angel in a burning bush, to lead his people out of captivity in the land of Egypt (Exodus 3:1,2). He emerged from the desert as a shepherd of a nation. When the people of Israel had been miraculously delivered from bondage in Egypt, the Lord led them through the wilderness on the way to the Promised Land. It was in the wilderness of Mt. Sinai that God spoke to them. He first spoke to Moses and then to them all, in a cloud of smoke and fire on Mt. Sinai. It was in the wilderness that God reached out to His people to establish a covenant relationship. He didn't deliver the people of Israel from the bondage of Egypt to send them on their merry way. He delivered them to become a nation unto Himself. Furthermore, before they would prosper in the land of milk and honey, God led them into the wilderness to meet Him there, wooing them unto Himself.

> I bore you on eagles' wings and brought you to Myself. Now therefore, if you will indeed obey My voice and keep My covenant, then you shall be a special treasure to Me...And you shall be to Me a kingdom of priests and a holy nation.
> —EXODUS 19:4-6

134

Again and again God miraculously provided for the people of Israel, proving his faithfulness and love towards them. He had saved them from the pursuit of the Egyptians as Moses exclaimed, "Do not be afraid, stand still and see the salvation of the Lord, . . . The Lord will fight for you, and you shall hold your peace" (Exodus 14:13-14). God sustained them by providing a dry path through the Red Sea and by submerging the Egyptian army in the sea. Furthermore, God continually provided water, bread, meat and a pillar of fire (Exodus 13:21, 16:12, 35, 17:6) to ensure their safety and faith in Him.

> And ye shall know that I am the Lord your God.
> —EXODUS 16:12

But the children of Israel repeatedly complained in unbelief. "Because of the contention of the children of Israel, and because they tempted the Lord, saying, 'Is the Lord among us or not?'" (Exodus 17:7). They also continually disobeyed God and broke His commandments. "And the Lord said to Moses, 'How long do you refuse to keep My commandments and My laws?'" (Exodus 16:28). Because of their unbelief and sin, the people of Israel wandered for many years. They not only wandered through an external wilderness but also through an inward desert, a barrenness of heart and soul.

However, Moses, the one whom God had called to lead them, continued to intercede on their behalf saying, "O Lord, let my Lord, I pray go among us, even though we are a stiff-necked people, and pardon our iniquity and our sin, and take us as Your inheritance" (Exodus 34:9). And God answered,

> My presence will go with you, and I will give you rest . . . Behold, I make a covenant. Before all your people I will do marvels such as have not been done in all the earth, nor in any nation; and all the people among whom you are shall see the work of the Lord . . . Observe what I command you this day . . . Take heed to yourself, lest you

135

make a covenant with the inhabitants of the land where you are going . . . But you shall destroy their altars . . . (for you shall worship no other god, for the Lord, whose name is Jealous, is a jealous God).

—EXODUS 33:14; 34:10-14

God used the wilderness to draw His people to Himself and to mold them to become a living testimony of God's grace, holiness and power to peoples of all nations.

This account of Israel's wandering in the wilderness is a dramatic manifestation of God's deliverance, grace and hope in a time of man's rebellion, desperation and unbelief. Indeed, in many ways it resembles our own wilderness experiences throughout our lives. Instead of drawing nigh to God, and seeking His presence, we turn our attention to all sorts of idols and momentary pleasures. Instead of trusting in God's provision, we murmur, and turn to our own strength or to forbidden means in order to provide. Are we only interested in the hand of God to provide the promised milk and honey, or are we yearning for a covenant relationship with God, whose name is Jealous? In the desert, He seeks to find us and waits for us to seek Him. Are we willing to meet Him in the desert of our lives? Are we willing to be stripped of all our earthly pomp and circumstance to come into His presence to seek His face and to embrace Him?

Seek the Lord and His strength;
Seek His face evermore.

—PSALM 105:4

When You said, "Seek My face,"
My heart said to You, "Your face, Lord, I will seek."

—PSALM 27:8

Surely, God wants to bless us with all kinds of earthly goods, but more than anything, He covets and commands that we love Him. Only when we come unreservedly into His presence can

He cause the deserts of our hearts and souls to flourish and to bloom. Only then can He turn our languishing into a testimony of His love, joy and power. Only then can the river of grace flow freely to quench our thirst and to give birth to new life.

> I will even make a road in the wilderness. And rivers in the desert ... To give drink to My people.
> —ISAIAH 43:19–20

> For the Lord will comfort Zion He will comfort all her waste places, He will make her wilderness like Eden, and her desert like the garden of the Lord; joy and gladness will be found in it, thanksgiving and the voice of melody.
> —ISAIAH 51:3

> For I have satiated the weary soul, and I have replenished every sorrowful soul.
> —JEREMIAH 31:25

As mentioned earlier, there are many different reasons why we may find ourselves in the wilderness. In order to seek God's presence in solitude and to be restored, we may need to intentionally forsake our comfortable but distracting surroundings. At times, God beckons us to meet Him in a personal desert created by relinquishing all that takes pre-eminence in our lives and that vies to take His place. But all too often in our daily lives, we find ourselves inevitably and hopelessly lost in a desert of the heart and soul. These deserts in our lives can be caused by external circumstances. They can also occur because of sin within our hearts and minds, regardless of outward conditions. They can occur during times of famine or plenty, of loss or gain or of pain or pleasure. Trauma, illness, disability, poverty, loss of loved ones, loss of employment and loss of a dream are some of the most common external causes that turn our hearts to inward places of wilderness and barrenness. It is in those deserts of the heart that God can meet us in a most profound and intimate way. However, in time of plenty, our own sin can have the same effect on our soul. Covetousness, lust for money, pleasure and success seem to be the norm of today's society. Yet, we don't realize how our love for God and for one another has waxed cold in the process. At the same time, we are progressively forsaking the basic Judeo-Christian values upon which this country was founded to follow the gods of secularism and relativism. Instead of pressing on to claim the Promised Land, we are regressing to live in the bondages of sin. Instead of appropriating God's deliverance, we are returning to an "Egypt" of the heart and mind—a state of slavery and ungodliness. We have become an adulterous, idolatrous people. Until we repent and return to God, our hearts and minds will succumb to and remain in a desert-like condition. Until we seek God anew, we shall wander in a spiritual wilderness as individuals and as a nation. How dry and deadly a desert do our hearts have to become before we cry out to meet God, who is a holy fire and whose name is Jealous?

There have been many experiences of inward wilderness in my life that prompted me to seek and find God's presence and help. Some were similar to one incident that occurred while I was traveling by car through the Death Valley desert on the way to San Diego. It was in the month of June. I was totally ignorant of the fact that this desert is below sea level and the temperatures rise above 120 degrees Fahrenheit. My car had no air-conditioning. Within one and a half hours of driving in seething temperatures, I anticipated fainting or maybe even dying of thirst in that forsaken place. I hadn't seen a single car or gas station in forty-five minutes. When I cried to the Lord in desperation, a cool air miraculously came over my whole body, and my thirst was totally quenched. I was so amazed and so comfortable that thirty minutes later I didn't even stop for water at the only gas station in sight. By His Spirit, God revived me and stilled my thirst, as He has so often restored me and quenched the thirst in my heart and soul.

God's presence is the answer in our times in the wilderness. He is there to meet us, to love us, to deliver us, to purify us and to turn us into a testimony of His grace and glory. In His love, He woos us to enter into a glorious covenant relationship with Him. He seeks us as individuals and as a people. This nation has many godly leaders. They intercede and are equipped and willing to lead us out of the "Egypt" in our hearts to meet God face to face in the wilderness. Then, we can enter the promised land of His kingdom. What will it take for us, as a nation and as individuals, to appropriate the deliverance available to us? What will it take for us to shed the chains of sin and, instead, become slaves of righteousness in God's kingdom? By the blood of His own Son, the Lamb of God, God has paid the price to free us from the slavery of sin and death. He has paid the price so we may become slaves of God and His righteousness.

> And having been set free from sin, you have become slaves of righteousness . . . having become slaves of God, you have your fruit to holiness, and the end everlasting life.
> —ROMANS 6:18, 22

Indeed, God not only paid the utmost price in order for us to become slaves of righteousness, but also to become His sons and heirs:

> But when the fullness of the time had come, God sent forth His Son . . . that we might receive the adoption as sons . . . and if a son, then an heir through Christ.
> —GALATIANS 4:4-5, 7

> Giving thanks to the Father who has qualified us to be partakers of the inheritance of the saints in the light. He has delivered us from the power of darkness and translated us into the kingdom of the son of His love.
> —COLOSSIANS 1:12-13

> When the Son of Man comes in His glory . . . then the
> king will say . . . "Come, you blessed of My Father, inherit
> the kingdom prepared for you from the foundation of
> the world."
> —MATTHEW 25:31, 34

To enter the promised land and to become heirs of God's kingdom, we must first accept His deliverance by grace, and depart from the kingdom of the world—the "Egypt" within us. Then it is only within the boundaries of a covenant relationship with God, as His sons and as slaves of His righteousness, that we may inherit and claim His glorious kingdom. What is God's kingdom?

> For the kingdom of God is not food and drink, but righteousness and peace and joy in the Holy Spirit.
> —ROMANS 14:17

How can we possibly turn down, ignore or wander away from so great an inheritance? The children of Israel, at times, lost their vision of the Promised Land and even wanted to go back to the slavery of Egypt. The apostle Paul observed similar tendencies in some disciples of his day.

> But now after you have known God, or rather are known by
> God, how is it that you turn again to the weak and beggarly
> elements, to which you desire again to be in bondage?
> —GALATIANS 4:9

How far we seem to wander from the freedom of the promised land of His righteousness. How often, even in our daily lives, we are tempted and fall again into the bondage of unbelief, idolatry and other sins. But, thanks be to God, by His grace, He continues to call us and to move us onward. He calls us as individuals and as a people, to be delivered from our bondage, to find Him in the deserts of our lives and to enter and claim anew His kingdom of righteousness, peace and joy. Let us heed His call. Let Him lead us into the promised land. Let Him be God.

God who calls you into His own kingdom and glory.
—1 THESSALONIANS 2:12

Let us encourage one another to seek God in our wilderness and to heed the voice of Him who is ever yearning to deliver us and lead us to our inheritance and the glory of His presence. Let us be available to help others to survive in, and to come out of the wilderness. During my own various episodes of "deserts" in my life, whether they were due to external circumstances, such as prolonged illness, bombing in World War II, divorce, childlessness, homelessness, abuse, neglect, loss of loved ones, or else due to inward struggles that came with tribulation and temptation, God responded to my cries by revealing Himself to me by His Spirit, by His Word and also by His people. Throughout the decades, God's people came my way to offer a drink of love and prayer to heal me from some of the agonizing pain of everyday living. They came in the name of Jesus to give me hope and to lead me to the arms of the Great Shepherd, in whose presence there is life and fullness of joy.

Let us be a spring of water and a cool shade to those who find themselves in a wilderness. Let us sacrifice some of our own comfort to meet them in the desert to give them drink and to share the Bread of Life. It is in the desert where we can encounter God in a most intimate way. It is in the desert that He sometimes calls us to go forth with a renewed vision, power and grace. Let us be willing to be sent into the wilderness to meet God, as well as to minister deliverance, hope, grace and new strength. Let us be willing to meet others in the deserts of their lives and to let God reveal Himself by way of His people.

Chapter 18

The Lion's Roar

ONE OF THE most difficult storms to weather in our hearts and minds is the turmoil and anguish that can be produced by anxiety, terror and fear—fear of loss or harm, fear of defeat and shame, fear of abandonment, fear of suffering and death, fear of fear itself. In the face of encounters with wickedness, sin and death in the world, we can feel threatened by the evils of Satan roaring like a lion. He is seeking to devour us as we tremble and are paralyzed with fear. Fortunately for those who abide in the fold of the Good Shepherd, Jesus rises like a lion, ready to defend His sheep.

With His staff He gently leads us; with His rod He pursues and strikes the enemy. Indeed, in face of our foe He rises up like a king and like a lion, ready to destroy his foe.

> I will meet them like a bear deprived of her cubs; I will tear open their rib cage, and there I will devour them like a lion. The wild beast shall tear them.
>
> —HOSEA 13:8

> Yea, though I walk through the valley of the shadow of death, I will fear no evil; for You are with me; Your rod and Your staff, they comfort me.
>
> —PSALM 23:4

In the summer of 1996 I revisited the charming town of Newport, Rhode Island. It just happened to be the day of a foreboding hurricane raging out at sea, off the New England shores. I ventured to climb the majestic rocks that rise from the ocean floor. I watched the waves elevate ten feet high, then overturn and descend with the force of Niagara Falls. In the fierceness of the storm and incoming tide, the ocean roared like a lion. Its rocks thrashed about on the ocean floor, resonated like drum rolls and the thunder of galloping horses. Approaching waves crashed and pounced with a symbolic bang upon the immovable rocks. They exploded into splendid arrays of white fountains dancing in joyful exhilaration and rising high in exaltation of the most high God. I trembled in awe and, at the same time, rejoiced at the greatness of our God and the power of His might.

> Oh, worship the Lord in the beauty of holiness!
> Tremble before Him, all the earth.
> Say among the nations, "The Lord reigns;
> The world also is firmly established,
> It shall not be moved;
> He shall judge the peoples righteously."
> Let the heavens rejoice, and let the earth be glad;
> Let the sea roar, and all its fullness.
> —PSALM 96:9–11

Somehow, in watching the fury of the sea, it was comforting to be reminded so vividly of the power of God. It was refreshing to be reminded that the God of the universe, who is a loving and just God, is in control and in power for all eternity. Indeed, He rises up like a lion to defend us and to destroy our enemies around us, as well as our self-made enemy—sin— within us.

> He will lift up a banner to the nations from afar, and will whistle to them from the end of the earth; surely they

143

shall come with speed, swiftly. In that day they will roar against them like the roaring of the sea.

—ISAIAH 5:26, 30

What a privilege it is to know that the God of the universe is a God who abundantly provides for us and rises up like a lion to protect us. He, in turn, expects us, His children and heirs of His kingdom, to acknowledge Him in all our ways and to pledge our allegiance to Him, the King of the Universe. Have we been too satisfied by God's abundance? Have we forgotten Him and His benefits? As individuals or as a nation, have we turned our backs on God in our rebellion, pride and complacency? God is a jealous God. He will not tolerate idolatry and rebellion for long, but will raise up a standard and purge our hearts from pride, pollution, self will, power and control. He will rise like a lion, ready to defend His rightful crown and territory within our hearts.

> Yet I am the Lord your God ever since the land of Egypt, and you shall know no God but Me; for there is no savior besides Me. I knew you in the wilderness, in the land of great drought. When they had pasture, they were filled; they were filled and their heart was exalted; therefore they forgot me. So I will be to them like a lion; like a leopard by the road I will observe them; I will meet them like a bear deprived of her cubs; I will tear open their rib cage, and there I will devour them like a lion. The wild beast shall tear them.
>
> —HOSEA 13:4-8

When we remove ourselves from God's presence and grace, we walk in sin; and sin produces fear. Only God can eliminate our fear, because God is love, and love casts out fear. As we are cleansed by the blood of the Lamb and empowered to walk in His grace, fear is replaced by confidence, trust and boldness. In Christ Jesus we can roar like the sea and remove those stumbling blocks of fear that have weighed us down at the bottom of our hearts. Then we can rejoice triumphantly in His freedom and His strength, and glorify God.

> He who does not love does not know God, for God is love . . . There is no fear in love; but perfect love casts out fear, because fear involves torment. But he who fears has not been made perfect in love.
>
> —1 JOHN 4:8, 18

> In whom we have boldness and access with confidence through faith in Him.
>
> —EPHESIANS 3:12

All too often we are weak and fail to immerse our hearts and minds in His Word. We fail to trust in Him to deliver us from evil—evil from outside of us, or evil from within. But God, in His tender mercy, delivers us from our distress and fear.

> I sought the Lord, and He heard me,
> And delivered me from all my fears.
>
> —PSALM 34:4

> The sorrows of Sheol surrounded me;
> The snares of death confronted me.
> In my distress I called upon the Lord, and cried out to
>   my God;
> He heard me from His temple,
> And my cry came before Him, even to his ears.
>
> —PSALM 18:5, 6

> Fear not, for I am with you; be not dismayed, for I am your God. I will strengthen you, yes I will help you, I will uphold you with My righteous right hand . . . For I, the Lord your God, will hold your right hand, Saying to you, "Fear not, I will help you."
>
> —ISAIAH 41:10, 13

One scary moment in my life occurred when I was sent by an agency to care for an elderly man. While I was cooking a meal, he grabbed the kitchen knife and held it up and pointed at my face. He was smiling so I couldn't tell whether he was joking or not. My heart pounded. I implored the protection of the Lord, and immediately, from deep within my soul, these words rose up and declared, "I praise you, Jesus. I praise you, Jesus."

He dropped the knife and asked, "What did you say?"

I replied and repeated, "Praise you Jesus."

Surprised, he remarked, "I'm holding a knife in your face, and you're praising Jesus?" In astonishment he shook his head and apologized for scaring me. He then proceeded to talk about long gone days of his childhood and time spent at Sunday School. I asked him if he wanted to take Jesus into his heart. He said he would think about it.

Another time, while on an airplane on its way across the Atlantic to the United States, God told me that there would be a fire on the plane. Fortunately, He also said not to worry because He would take care of it. Sure enough, half way across the ocean, one engine caught on fire. As the pilot graciously and calmly announced this on the intercom, the passengers were quite alarmed. I wasn't sure whether or not to say anything, so I simply prayed. Within twenty minutes the captain announced, "We have the fire under control and are able to make an emergency landing in Newfoundland, where we can switch planes." Throughout this ordeal I was as calm as could be because of what God had spoken. His Word quieted the lion's roar of bad tidings and shielded me from reacting to its terror. His Word had protected me from an onslaught of fear and had given me peace and confidence.

> He will not be afraid of evil tidings;
> His heart is steadfast, trusting in the Lord.
>
> —PSALM 112:7

> My son, let them not depart from your eyes—
> Keep sound wisdom and discretion . . .

146

When you lie down, you will not be afraid;
Yes, you will lie down and your sleep will be sweet.
Do not be afraid of sudden terror,
Nor of trouble from the wicked when it comes;
For the Lord will be your confidence,
And will keep your foot from being caught.

—PROVERBS 3:21, 24–26

You shall not be afraid of the terror by night,
Nor of the arrow that flies by day.

—PSALM 91:5

When we abide in God's Word and remain within the boundaries of His kingdom, Christ our great Shepherd rises like a lion, ready to defend His sheep and to subdue every enemy.

He enables us to quiet our hearts and to remain steadfast and unmoved in the face of great danger, terror and tragedy.

Are we, as individuals, families, communities and as a nation, willing to humble ourselves and pray for the Prince of Peace to conquer our sins and fears within us? Are we willing to turn to the God of the universe who, alone, can still every fear and defeat every foe?

In humility and in the fear of the Lord, our fears will cease. Our trials and traumas will turn into triumph. Our tragedies will turn into trophies of great courage, hope and heroic love. Our mourning will turn into a song of promised comfort and victory. Our wounded hearts will reach for the hand that holds the oil of healing. Our pain will turn into prayer to beseech the resurrection power of the One who is invincible. Our fears will turn to faith in the One who sits on the throne and is ever ready to defend His people.

In the beginning of the twenty-first century, Americans and people around the world need to give their all in order to become partakers of the victory that is available in the majestic name of Jesus, the Lord triumphant. We must let go of pride and prejudice, rebellion and greed, unbelief and ungodliness in

147

order to embrace the power and glory of the Lord Most High.

Christ laid down His life for us so that we may share in His triumph. What price are we willing to pay to heed His call to humble ourselves and seek His face? Let us heed His call to humbly approach the throne of God that He may answer our cry for deliverance and healing.

> But whoever listens to me will dwell safely,
> And will be secure, without fear of evil.
>
> —PROVERBS 1:33

> Because he has set his love upon Me ... I will answer him ... I will deliver him ...
>
> —PSALM 91:14,15

> If My people who are called by My name will humble themselves and pray and seek My face, and turn from their wicked ways, then I will hear from heaven, and will forgive their sin and heal their land.
>
> —2 CHRONICLES 7:14

In humility and repentance we find God's deliverance. In humility, Christ, the spotless Lamb of God, was slain for our sins. In great victory and glory, He arose as the Lion of Judah. As Christ has prevailed over the power of darkness and death, we, who are washed by the blood of the Lamb, may rise in His triumph and glory.

> Worthy is the Lamb who was slain, to receive power ... and honor and glory ... Behold, the Lion of the tribe of Judah ... has prevailed.
>
> —REVELATION 5:12, 5

> When the enemy comes like a flood, the Spirit of the Lord will lift up a standard against him ... Arise, shine ... the Lord will arise over you, and His glory will be seen upon you.
>
> —ISAIAH 59:19; 60: 1, 2

CHAPTER 19

THRONE

A S WE STRUGGLE through the valleys and enjoy the high peaks of our lives, we sometimes forget that our final destination is the throne of God. Whether we are in the desert or in the depth of the sea, in green pastures or on the mountaintops, God seeks to rule in our hearts and minds. In any of our circumstances He desires for us to seek Him, to trust Him, to fellowship with Him, to worship and to serve Him who sits on the throne and rules over heaven and earth. Our inner voyage to the throne of God is a voyage ordained by His grace. He beckons us to come near and to call Him "abba," or "Father," so that He may bestow upon us the crown of life and the crown of glory.

> Blessed is the man who endures temptation, for when he has proved, he will receive the crown of life which the Lord has promised to those who love Him.
>
> —JAMES 1:12

> And when the Chief Shepherd appears, you will receive the crown of glory that does not fade away.
>
> —1 PETER 5:4

By grace we are invited and called to approach the throne of God on a daily basis. By grace we are promised to see Him face to face upon Christ's return. As kingdoms and nations on earth appear and disappear, diminish and expand, the whole world is being shaped to set the stage for Christ's triumphant return, in all His glory and in all His might.

> Then they will see the Son of Man coming in a cloud with power and great glory.
>
> —LUKE 21:27

> And the dead in Christ shall rise first.
>
> —1 THESSALONIANS 4:16

> ... but the throne of God and of the Lamb shall be in it, and His servants shall serve Him. They shall see His face ...
>
> —REVELATION 22:3-4

Are we preparing our hearts and minds daily to meet Him face to face? "For now we see in a mirror, dimly, but then face to face" (1 Cor. 13:12). Are we longing to see Him, the King of glory? As we weather the storms in our life's journey, let us not only seek His hand, but let us hold fast to our faith in anticipation of seeing Him face to face. Let us allow His hand to save us and to guide us on our voyage to approach the throne of God.

The only way we can approach the throne of God is by abandoning our own thrones. As long as we remain on our own self-appointed thrones, in control of our thoughts, feelings and actions, apart from Christ, we are traveling away from God's presence and grace towards inevitable death.

> The sinful passions ... were at work in our members to bear fruit to death.
>
> —ROMANS 7:5

> For to be carnally minded is death.
>
> —ROMANS 8:6

For the wages of sin is death.

—ROMANS 6:23

Christ was willing to relinquish His throne of glory, while He hung on the cross to pay the ransom for our sins with His own blood. By His blood we are reconciled to God and are made free to depart our throne which is built of corruptions of all kinds.

That you put off concerning your former conduct, the old man which grows according to the deceitful lust.

—EPHESIANS 4:22

By His blood, we are delivered from our slavery to sin, in order to become servants of righteousness.

And having been set free from sin, you became slaves of righteousness.

—ROMANS 6:18

But now having been set free from sin and having become slaves of God, you have your fruit to holiness, and the end, everlasting life.

—ROMANS 6:22

Christ was willing to humble Himself and to serve mankind with the ultimate sacrifice of giving His own life. Are we willing to humble ourselves and depart from our self-made thrones in order to become servants of His righteousness? Are we willing to present our bodies as a living and holy sacrifice, in honor of His name? It is only in surrendering to His will and in serving in His name that we may have true fellowship with Him. Only as we approach the throne of God and become true worshippers and servants of the Most High God may we rule with Him in His holiness and grace, glory and wisdom, power and might.

If we endure, we shall also reign with Him.
> —2 TIMOTHY 2:12

... and have redeemed us to God by Your blood ... and have made us kings and priests to our God, and we shall reign on the earth.
> —REVELATION 5:9-10

The voyage from our self-made thrones to the throne of God has been paid in full by the blood of the Lamb. The cross of Calvary is the only bridge between the two, and His Word is the holy fire that burns away every trace of our sinful past. His Word is the fire that consumes the strongholds of our thrones and lights the way to the throne of God. Are we willing to relinquish our self-constructed thrones and accept the lordship of Christ in our hearts and minds? If so, He may bestow upon us the blessings of His kingdom. As long as we impose our own wills upon our lives, apart from the will of God, our journey on the earth is a journey of vanity in the kingdom of darkness to eternal death. Do we desire to live and to seek the Giver of life? Do we hear His call and heed His royal command to embark on the voyage ordained by His grace that leads to His throne of eternal glory?

> ... all is vanity and grasping for the wind.
>
> All the labor is for the mouth,
> And yet the soul is not satisfied.
>
> I know that whatever God does,
> It shall be forever ...
> God does it, that men should fear before Him.
>
> Fear God and keep His commandments,
> For this is man's all.
>
> He has made everything beautiful in its time. Also He has put eternity in their hearts ... I know that nothing is better for them than to rejoice, and to do good in their lives.
> —ECCLESIASTES 1:14; 6:7; 3:14; 12:13; 3:11-12

CHAPTER 20

CROWN OF THORNS, CROWN OF GLORY

IN THE SUMMER of 1999, I had again the great fortune of returning to Newport, Rhode Island for a few weeks of vacation. I was received with a royal welcome by my Christian friends with whom I enjoyed a bond that grew deeper in the love of Christ as the years went by.

On the 4th of July, I visited a church in Worcester, Massachusetts. The congregation consisted of people from various nations and continents around the world. After a time of exuberant worship and praise to God, we thanked God for having sent His Son Jesus Christ, the King of Kings, to die on the cross to set us free from sin and eternal death. We also thanked God for all those who were willing to lay down their lives for this nation's liberty and justice for all. In the evening, I was gripped with a sense of history while watching a telecast presenting the Boston Pops Orchestra giving its seventieth free Independence Day concert to the public on the shore of the Charles River. I listened to the eloquent speech of Senator Edward Kennedy. Almost a half a million people participated in this marvelous celebration of this country's freedom. Many had waited all afternoon in scorching 100 degree heat to ensure a good place to view the evening's fireworks. The magnificent fireworks were skillfully synchronized to the orchestra's music.

153

The following day, I escaped the intense heat wave by crossing the Newport Bridge to watch the fireworks displayed from the shores of Newport. They were cast into the starry sky from Fort Adams, a magnificent stone structure that was built to replace the original fortification. The original fortification had been dedicated, in 1799, to then President of the United States, John Adams. It had fallen into disrepair while defending American soil from British attack during the short War of 1812. This new fortification was built between 1824 and 1857 and served in coastal defense through World War II.

Now, hundreds of people—many on ships and boats—had gathered to observe this festive celebration commemorating America's Declaration of Independence and the many victories won in defending her freedom. It was exciting to listen to the children's ooh's and aah's as we watched a myriad of designs exploding in the night sky above and reflecting in the water below. At the end, the people clapped, and many ships and boats sounded their horns and bells in various pitches. They expressed appreciation for the fireworks display and for the joy that freedom brings.

On this occasion, there were some unusual designs in the fireworks—formations that depicted stars and planets, fountains and torches. There was one in the form of a cross surrounded by a circle of fire. *How appropriate,* I thought. There was a price paid, in blood, to form and protect this Union, a young nation free to explore and exercise liberty and justice for all. There was a price paid, in blood, to free the slaves of this land. Most of all, there was a price paid, in blood, to set man free. It was Jesus' death on the cross of Calvary that paid the price to set us free from the slavery of sin. It was the shed blood of Jesus that made us free to know, to worship and to serve, God. It was the cross that unites us believers to become a holy nation unto God, a holy temple in the Lord and a dwelling place of God.

But you are chosen generation, a royal priesthood, a holy nation, His own special people, that you may proclaim the praises of Him who called you out of darkness into His marvelous light.

—1 PETER 2:9

Jesus Christ Himself being the chief cornerstone, in whom the whole building, being joined together, grows into a holy temple in the Lord, in whom you also are being built together for a dwelling place—of God in the Spirit.

—EPHESIANS 2:20-22

This country once called itself a nation under God, seeking God's blessings and benefits as we acknowledged His lordship. We fought wars and implored God's power, wisdom and protection. In this decade, however, more than ever before, this nation exhibits a departure from the truth we once labeled as self-evident. Who or what has become the lord of this nation? How long can freedom ring, when we recklessly forsake the truth that sets us free?

Let us learn from the Scriptures and the warnings of God in sight of Israel's wayward people and kings. In the first book of Samuel we find Israel tremendously blessed under Samuel's leadership. After having taken possession of the promised land, Israel continued to prosper and to triumph in each war, as long as they allowed God to be their King.

So the children of Israel said to Samuel, "Do not cease to cry out to the Lord our God for us, that He may save us from the hand of the Philistines." . . . So the Philistines were subdued, and they did not come anymore into the territory of Israel. And the hand of the Lord was against the Philistines all the days of Samuel. Then the cities which the Philistines had taken from Israel were restored to Israel.

—1 SAMUEL 7:8, 13-14

155

But when Samuel was old, his sons took his place. They did not walk in God's ways. Instead of beseeching God for His leadership, they insisted on crowning a king. Moreover, they insisted on crowning a king of their own choice.

> Nevertheless the people refused to obey the voice of Samuel; and they said, "No, but we will have a king over us, that we also may be like all nations, and that our king may judge us and go out before us and fight our battles."
>
> —1 Samuel 8:19-20

They chose Saul to be their king in spite of the instructions and warnings of the Lord.

> And the Lord said to Samuel, "Heed the voice of the people in all that they say to you; for they have not rejected you, but they have rejected Me, that I should not reign over them . . . However, you shall solemnly forewarn them, and show them the behavior of the king who will reign over them."
>
> —1 Samuel 8:7, 9

> So Samuel told all the words of the Lord to the people who asked him for a King, and he said, "And you will cry out in that day because of your king whom you have chosen for yourselves, and the Lord will not hear you in that day."
>
> —1 Samuel 8:10-11, 18

> So the people went to Gilgal, and there they made Saul king before the Lord in Gilgal.
>
> —1 Samuel 11:15

Even though God communicated His disapproval of the newly chosen king, in His mercy, He was still willing to bless Israel as long as the people and the king obeyed His voice.

> If you fear the Lord and serve Him and obey His voice and do not rebel against the commandment of the Lord, then both of you and the king who reigns over you will

continue following the Lord your God. However, if you do not obey the voice of the Lord, but rebel against the commandment of the Lord, then the hand of the Lord will be against you, as it was against your fathers.

—1 SAMUEL 12:14-15

Only fear the Lord, and serve Him in truth with all your heart; for consider what great things He has done for you. But if you still do wickedly you shall be swept away, both you and your king.

—1 SAMUEL 12:24-25

Saul had reigned for only two years over Israel when he decided to attack the Philistines, engulfing the Israelites in great defeat and distress. To make matters worse, he arranged peace offerings and a burnt offering, a form of worship, without complying with the ordinances of God. When Samuel came and saw this, he was distraught and prophesied,

> And Samuel said to Saul, "You have done foolishly. You have not kept the commandment of the Lord your God, which He commanded you. For now the Lord would have established your kingdom over Israel forever. But now your kingdom shall not continue. The Lord has sought for Himself a man after HIS own heart, and the Lord commanded him to be a commander over His people, because you have not kept what the Lord commanded you."

—1 SAMUEL 13:13-14

But Saul continued to reign in his own way, to wage war in his own way and to worship in his own way (1 Sam. 15:18-19,22,24,26,28). Moreover, when he realized David's superior triumphs in battle, he was exceedingly jealous and sought to kill him. In this process Saul even killed a number of priests and destroyed an entire city (1 Sam. 22:17, 23:8,10). Finally, God intervened and put an end to Saul's strivings. Saul and Israel were virtually destroyed at the hand of the Philistines, allowing the Philistines to dwell in their land.

> So the Philistines fought against Israel; and the men of
> Israel fled from before the Philistines and fell slain on
> Mount Gilboa . . . So Saul, his three sons, his armor bearer,
> and all his men died together that same day.
>
> —1 SAMUEL 31:1, 6

> And when the men of Israel who were on the other side
> of the valley and . . . on the other side of the Jordan, saw
> that Saul and his sons were dead, they forsook the cities
> and fled; and the Philistines came and dwelt in them.
>
> —1 SAMUEL 31:7

But all was not lost. God had already appointed and
anointed David, a man after God's heart, to lead His people out
of great disaster and into prosperity and triumph.

> So David inquired of the Lord . . . And He answered him,
> "Pursue, for you shall surely overtake them and without
> fail recover all."
>
> —1 SAMUEL 30:8

Like Moses, David allowed God to triumph in battle. Like
Moses, David led the people to heed God's ordinances and to
look to God for their salvation.

> The Lord your God has given you this land to possess. You
> must not fear them, for the Lord your God Himself fights
> for you.
>
> —DEUTERONOMY 3:20, 22

As long as King David and his people followed God's commands and trusted God as their salvation, Israel triumphed,
again, to possess and to prosper in its promised land. It was a
cycle that was to repeat itself many times throughout the
history of Israel and of mankind. It was a cycle similar to one
we may exhibit in our daily journey through life. It is a cycle
of transition from a state of well-being under God's reign to a
state of destruction and futility because of our rebellion.

Finally, it ends in appropriating God's offer and provision of grace and restoration.

God is continually calling to restore us unto a relationship with Him as King of our hearts and minds. He is seeking to restore His kingdom within us. As we journey away from God, through the slavery of unbelief and sin and the wilderness of rebellion, He calls us to embrace the miracle of *His* grace and restoration. By faith in *His* grace, He restores us to repossess our own "promised land." What is our "promised land"? It is a covenant relationship with God, where we eternally abide in His presence and grace and inherit His glorious kingdom.

> For the kingdom of God is not food and drink, but righteousness and peace and joy in the Holy Spirit.
> —ROMANS 14:17

> Then Peter said to them, "Repent, and let everyone of you be baptized in the name of Jesus Christ for the remission of sins; and you shall receive the gift of the Holy Spirit. For the promise is to you and to your children, and to all who are a far off . . . "
> —ACTS 2:38-39

> This is the covenant that I will make with them. I will put My laws into their hearts, and in their minds will I write them. Their sins I will remember no more.
> —HEBREWS 10:16-17

> And this is the promise that He has promised us—eternal life.
> —1 JOHN 2:25

> And if you are Christ's then you are heirs according to the promise.
> —GALATIANS 3:29

Are we walking in His statutes as heirs of the eternal kingdom of God? Is He King of our hearts and minds? Do we let

Him reign in our thoughts and actions? Do we let Him wage our wars His way? Do we worship as He commands?

> God is Spirit, and those who worship Him must worship in spirit and in truth.
>
> —JOHN 4:24

How often and how long do we have to do things our way before we realize that we have strayed far from God? How many idols and carnal kings do we have to trust and serve before we realize that the end result is barrenness, death and pain? In spite of God's numerous warnings, we, like the Israelites, take detours in our daily lives, giving homage in our thoughts and actions to rulers of the carnal realm. Sometimes we wander far away from God's promised kingdom within us, before we cry out and heed His call to be restored.

I had been a Christian for many years before I realized that I had never totally given my mind to the rulership of the Lord Jesus Christ. First I had given my heart to Him. Then, progressively, I gave Him my hands, to do as He pleased; my feet, to go where He wanted me to go; my ears, to hear what He wanted me to hear, and my mouth, to speak what He wanted me to say. But my mind was a different matter. For some reason that was, and still is, the most difficult aspect of my walk with God to surrender to Him. I had yearned and learned to walk, talk, hear and do His Word as best as I could. In the course of several decades, I made occasional detours by straying from God's will but was always repenting and returning to God to restore my relationship with Him.

However, the journey of my mind seemed to have a course of its own. On a daily basis, I found it easier to put my actions under the discipline of the Lord than my thoughts. Even though I sincerely desired to grow in the knowledge of the Lord Jesus Christ, I was far from allowing Him to rule in all the secret places of my mind. It wasn't until I came to another crisis in my life, during which my thoughts turned dark and bitter, that I realized I desperately needed help. In a frantic search for a comforting, strengthening word from God, I found and grasped this lifesaving verse:

> For the weapons of our warfare are not carnal but mighty in God for pulling down strongholds, casting down arguments and every high thing that exalts itself against the knowledge of God bringing every thought into captivity to the obedience of Christ.
> —2 CORINTHIANS 10:4-5

The words every thought not only caught my attention, but convicted me deeply. I realized that my battle wasn't only in my circumstances but, indeed, within myself. I also realized that it wasn't a battle for me to win, but that the battle was the Lord's, and the victory had already been won on the cross of Calvary. Christ had worn a crown of thorns when he was crucified. His head was bruised and wounded so that my thoughts could be set free. I was no longer a prisoner of my thoughts, but free to seek deliverance and empowered to rise above my darkness.

> Seek the Lord while He may be found, call upon Him while He is near. Let the wicked forsake his way, and the unrighteousness man his thoughts; let him return to the Lord. And He will have mercy on him; and to our God, for He will abundantly pardon.
> —ISAIAH 55:6-7

> For My thoughts are not your thoughts, nor are your ways My ways, says the Lord. For as the heavens are higher than the earth, so are My ways higher than your ways, and My thoughts than your thoughts.
> —ISAIAH 55:8-9

During the July 4th fireworks exhibition, I was impressed by the formation of the encircled cross, as well as the formation

161

of the encircled stars. The encircled stars reminded me of the headpiece of the Statue of Liberty which I had enthusiastically viewed, for the first time, as a teenager while entering the New York harbor on an ocean liner. It was a thrilling sight to behold this "lady with the torch" that represented freedom. But it wasn't until now that I wondered about and appreciated all those who had laid down their lives for liberty to rule in this land. It wasn't until now that I appreciated the immense cost in human lives necessary, not only to birth, but to protect and defend again and again a nation with liberty and justice for all. There was a price paid, in human blood, for us to abide in this land of liberty.

Even more importantly there was a price paid, in blood, by the spotless Lamb of God to set our hearts and minds free. It was paid so we could abide in His kingdom, to worship Him in spirit and in truth and to enjoy the liberty of heart, mind and soul only found in Him. He paid the price to be our King, to free us from the slavery of sin, and to make us heirs of His kingdom. While Christ wore a crown of thorns, His blood covered His head, His heart, His body, His hands and feet. He had surrendered His will, His actions and His thoughts into the Father's hands. "Yet it pleased the Lord to bruise Him ... Because He poured out His soul unto death, ... and He bore the sins of many ... " (Is. 53: 10, 12).

But His crown of thorns was replaced by a crown of glory. His crown of glory will forever consist of the people of His kingdom—those whom He had purchased with His own blood, who will trust in Him and reflect His glory and His resurrection power.

> The Gentiles shall see your righteousness, and all the Kings of your glory ... You shall also be a crown of glory in the hand of the Lord, and a royal diadem in the hand of your God.
>
> —ISAIAH 62:2-3

In turn, He, who is the king of glory, will forever be a crown of glory to His people.

> Who is this King of Glory?
> The Lord strong and mighty.
> The Lord mighty in battle.
> Who is this King of Glory?
> The Lord of hosts.
> He is the King of Glory.
>
> —PSALM 24:8, 10

> In that day the Lord of hosts will be for a crown of glory
> and a diadem of beauty to the remnant of His people.
> —ISAIAH 28:5

Shall we be His crown of glory and let Him be our King? Or shall we, in our daily lives, choose other kings and gods? Shall we let Christ rule in our hearts and cleanse our thoughts, or shall we crucify Him anew by serving other gods and idols?

What are some of our carnal rulers that we follow? They are often unbelief, rebellion, fear, greed, hypocrisy and lust. Sometimes they appear as desirable acts of righteousness but are not ordained by God. Many wars were waged in the name of Christ, but not planned by God. Many religions were born of man, not birthed by the breath of God. Man has a tendency to do things his own way. In so doing, he inevitably breaks God's laws and separates himself from God's rulership and benefits. Are we waging our wars our own way? Are we serving and worshiping God our own way? Our quality of worship is affected by our thoughts and actions. Conversely, our thoughts and actions are affected by our quality of worship. Are our thoughts, desires and plans born out of the ordinances of God, or are they contrived out of the carnal mind? The consequences of a carnal and evil mind are severe. Even the thoughts and plans that seem right to man, but are contrary to

163

the counsel of God, eventually lead to destruction and death. They are born of corruptible seed, in enmity with God and are an abomination in His sight.

> There is a way that seems right to a man,
> But its end is the way of death.
>   —PROVERBS 14:12

> The wicked in his proud countenance does not seek God;
> God is in none of his thoughts.
>   —PSALM 10:4

> The thoughts of the wicked are an abomination to the Lord.
>   —PROVERBS 15:26

> Do you not know that friendship in the world is enmity with God?
>   —JAMES 4:4

It is of utmost importance that we submit to God's rulership while we can, while He offers grace and restoration to a repentant heart and mind. Even God's mercy has its limits when His wisdom and rulership are continually denied.

> Because I have called and you refused,
> I have stretched our my hand and no one regarded...
>
> Then they will call on me, but I will not answer...
> Because they hated knowledge and did not choose the
>   fear of the Lord,
> They would have none of my counsel
> And despised my every rebuke.
>
> But whoever listen to me will dwell safely,
> And will be secure, without fear of evil.
>   —PROVERBS 1:24, 28-29, 33

Let us seek God while He may be found. Let us seek His knowledge and wisdom, and be restored to Him while He graciously calls us to let Him be the King of our lives. The benefits of heeding His counsel are numerous.

> Do not be wise in our own eyes;
> Fear the Lord and depart from evil.
> It will be health to your flesh,
> And strength to your bones.
>
> —PROVERBS 3:7

> The fear of the LORD is the beginning of knowledge,
> But fools despise wisdom and instruction.
>
> —PROVERBS 1:7

> A wise man will hear and increase in learning,
> And a man of understanding will attain wise counsel.
>
> —PROVERBS 1:5

> For the LORD gives wisdom;
> From His mouth come knowledge and understanding...
> He is a shield to those who walk uprightly...
> He guards the paths of justice,
> And preserves to the way of His saints.
>
> —PROVERBS 2:6–8

> Happy is the man who finds wisdom...
> Length of days is in her right hand,
> In her left hand riches and honor.
> ...And all her paths are peace.

> A crown of glory she will deliver you.
>
> —PROVERBS 3:13, 16–17; 4:9

Shall we be foolish, and follow idols who have nothing to offer but temporary gain or pleasure and inevitable destruction? Or shall we be crucified with Christ, who wore a crown of thorns, so that our foolishness can be washed away and be replaced by a crown of glory, righteousness and life.

> ...fools die for lack of wisdom.
> ...but righteousness delivers from death.
>
> —PROVERBS 10:21; 11:4

> Finally, there is laid up for me the crown of righteousness.
> —2 TIMOTHY 4:8

> Blessed is the man who endures temptation; for when he has been proved, he will receive the crown of life which the Lord has promised to those who love him.
> —JAMES 1:12

There is a transformation that takes place when we journey, by God's power and grace, from the kingdom of darkness to the kingdom of God's light in the knowledge of His Son. When Christ laid down His life for us He became the bridge that enables us to cross over the troubled waters of sin. We can now enter confidently into His realm, where truth and freedom reigns. Indeed, we are not only called to cross that bridge of forgiveness and renewal, but we are commanded to be transformed.

> And do not be conformed to this world, but be transformed by the renewing of your mind.
> —ROMANS 12:2

> And be renewed in Spirit of your mind.
> —EPHESIANS 4:23

> And have put on the new man who is renewed in knowledge according to the image of Him who created Him.
> —COLOSSIANS 3:10

This process of transformation also calls for purification and cleansing. While visiting a number of New England's lighthouses, I read about each one's history. I learned that in the early days the keeper of the lighthouse diligently cleaned the light in which the oil was burning. It was crucial to keep the oil's black smoke washed away, each day, to ensure the brilliancy and effectiveness of the light that saved many lives from perishing at sea. Jesus, the keeper of our souls, diligently seeks to wash us clean in our hearts, as well as in our minds.

> Finally, brethren ... whatever things are pure ... meditate on these things.
> —PHILIPPIANS 4:8

> But the wisdom that is from above is first pure ...
> —JAMES 3:17

> Since you have purified your souls in obeying the truth ...
> —1 PETER 1:22

> How much more shall the blood of Christ purge your conscience from dead works to serve the living God?
> —HEBREWS 9:14

Like a diamond in the rough, God is eager to fashion us into His image. He desires to cleanse us by the blood of His Son, Jesus Christ. He commands us to be transformed by the renewal of our minds. Shall we become His crown of glory, a diadem in His hand and a lighthouse that sends a pure and bright light in the storms and nights to those around us?

Another reason why it is of utmost importance to have our minds renewed in Christ is that, as we become more and more like Him and one with Him, we also become more and more unified with one another. Only in our individual union with Him can the Body of Christ become unified. Christ shed His blood for us, individually, but also for the sake of the Body of Christ, as a whole. The body of believers often struggles to maintain its clear identity, while Christians around the world are far from being unified. But the day is drawing closer when Christians from all walks of life and from many nations shall serve and worship with one accord.

> Be perfectly joined together in the same mind.
> —1 CORINTHIANS 1:10

167

> Be like-minded toward one another, according to Christ
> Jesus, that you may with one mind and one mouth glorify
> the God and Father of our Lord Jesus Christ.
> —ROMANS 15:5-6

> Endeavoring to keep the unity of the Spirit in the bond of
> peace.
> —EPHESIANS 4:3

It is crucial to be united in Christ's love as families, as communities and as the Body of Christ. We must unite in order to repossess, claim and defend the promised land available to us by faith in Christ. A house divided cannot stand. Nor can a kingdom divided withstand the attacks of an adversary. The more we are unified with Christ, the more we can be one-minded and unified with one another. The winds and tides of man's philosophies are changing in this country and around the world. Various wars of thought and weaponry lurk in hidden places. Because of this, the Body of Christ needs to unite and to seek one-mindedness in Christ to stand strong in the face of adversity.

Every war that was won to ensure liberty in this land was won because men, as well as women, united to fight for its freedom. They were united in vision, in candor, in commitment and in the willingness to lay down their lives for their goal. What will it take for believers around the world to become a united front and fortification to withstand the onslaughts against the kingdom of God? Are we willing to pay the price in order to unite and defend the freedom of our hearts and minds that was wrought on Calvary? Are we willing to defend, at all cost, the shores of the kingdom of God within us? By faith in Christ's forgiving blood, we journeyed across the sea of sin. By faith we stepped on the shores of Christ's kingdom. Let us, together as a holy nation, pledge allegiance and be faithful to our King, the King of Kings, whose faithfulness and goodness endures forever, and who is our crown of glory.

CHAPTER 21

CITIZENS OF TRIUMPH AND GRACE

THE DESIRED RESTORATION and unity of the Body of Christ, as mentioned in the previous chapter, depends greatly on the allegiance and loyalty of its individual members to Christ. A kingdom cannot stand united without the loyalty of the king to his subjects, nor without the loyalty of the subjects to the king. Any degree of betrayal, whether within a kingdom, a nation, a community or a family, can have devastating effects. But faithfulness, loyalty and commitment restore and ensure welfare. They are the most substantial ingredients of love and the most assuring characteristics of God. Because of God's faithfulness to us, He enables us, by the shed blood of His Son, to cross the sea of sin and to complete the voyage ordained by His grace. Because of God's faithfulness we can enter His presence and be restored and transformed into His image. Because of His faithfulness we can enter His kingdom and become loyal citizens of His kingdom.

God's kingdom is a kingdom of triumph because Christ is the King triumphant. Only in appropriating God's faithfulness and in becoming loyal citizens of His kingdom can we triumph over sin, death and darkness. Christ was faithful unto death, enduring the cross. Because of His loyalty to the Father, we inherited citizenship in His kingdom. Because of Christ's loyalty, we are empowered to triumph in Him.

169

Now thanks be to God who always leads us to triumph
in Christ.

—2 CORINTHIANS 2:14

What price are we willing to pay to become loyal citizens of
triumph? Are we willing to turn from our rebellion that occurs
in many fashions throughout our daily lives? Do we repent
when our thoughts and actions betray Christ? It is crucial that,
in order to triumph in Christ, we as individuals, families, communities and as a nation repent and commit ourselves daily to
appropriate God's characteristic of faithfulness. We need to
restore our loyalty to one another and to Him whose faithfulness endures forever. Only in allegiance to Christ can we be
fully united, restored and transformed to fulfill His purposes.

One of God's purposes of restoring the Body of Christ is to
restore and to build His holy temple.

For you are the temple of the living God.

—2 CORINTHIANS 6:16

Do you not know that you are the temple of God and that
the Spirit of God dwells in you? If anyone defiles the temple of God, God will destroy him. For the temple of God is
holy, which temple you are.

—1 CORINTHIANS 3:16-17

It is an awesome and humbling thought that we, who faithfully trust and abide in Him, are created and restored to be His temple and His dwelling place. We are being restored and built into a
holy temple in which His glory resides and is made manifest.

Having been built on the foundation of the apostles and
prophets, Jesus Christ Himself being the chief cornerstone,
in whom the whole building, being fitted together, grows
into a holy temple in the Lord, in whom you also are being
built together for a dwelling place of God in the Spirit.

—EPHESIANS 2:20-22

Indeed, God will not rest until He has completed the restoration of His temple. Shall we surrender to the workmanship of His power and grace, and allow Him to construct a temple fit for His glory and rest?

> For Zion's sake I will not hold my peace. And for Jerusalem's sake I will not rest, until her righteousness goes forth as brightness, And her salvation as a lamp that burns.
> —Isaiah 62:1

God will not rest until we appropriate the finished work of His Son's death on the cross and enter His rest. He, who is faithful, is calling His bride to turn from adultery to seek His face and to declare Her love to Him who is eternally faithful. God is calling His people to turn from idolatry and to serve and worship Him. He is calling a people to embark on the journey ordained by His grace and to enter His kingdom. It is a journey paid in full by the blood of the Lamb so we may become citizens of His kingdom of freedom and truth and of everlasting glory and rest.

> Therefore, holy brethren, partakers of the heavenly calling...
>
> Do not harden your hearts as in the rebellion...
>
> And to whom did He swear that they would not enter His rest, but to those who did not obey? So we see that they could not enter in because of unbelief.
>
> There remains therefore a rest to the people of God... Let us therefore be diligent to enter that rest, lest anyone fall according to the same example of disobedience.
> —Hebrews 3:1, 8, 18–19, 4:9, 11

Entering into God's glorious presence and rest is the ultimate triumph for us, individually and for the Body of Christ, corporately. Whether we journey through deserts, fires, floods

171

or valleys, or cross over mountaintops or a turbulent sea, whether we run through enemy territory or face violent storms, God's faithful hand is there to save us. It is there to guide us and to secure our inheritance in His kingdom as citizens of His triumph and grace.

> For You Lord, have made me glad through Your work;
> I will triumph in the works of Your hands.
> —PSALM 92:4

> Oh, clap your hands, all you peoples!
> Shout to God with the voice of triumph!
> For the Lord Most High is awesome;
> He is great King over all the earth.
> ... He will choose our inheritance for us.
> —PSALM 47:1-2, 4

The process of restoration and triumphant entrance into God's rest occurs also by a continual increase in the knowledge of God.

> ... and have put on the new man who is renewed in knowledge according to the image of Him who created Him.
> —COLOSSIANS 3:10

> That you may walk worthy of the Lord, fully pleasing Him, being fruitful in every good work and increasing in the knowledge of God.
> —COLOSSIANS 1:10

> ... that you may be filled with the knowledge of His will in all wisdom and spiritual understanding.
> —COLOSSIANS 1:9

Increasing in the knowledge of God is not only crucial in restoring and building the Temple of God, but it is vital in the development of our love for and faithfulness to Him, who is

172

the King of glory. It is impossible to truly love and be loyal to someone whom we do not know. Nor can one's love and loyalty toward someone grow deeper without knowing that individual more and more. Sometimes our increase in knowing and loving someone is hindered by our own blindness and rebellion. In order for us to grow in the knowledge and love of God, we need to surrender our hearts and minds to Him whose thoughts are higher than our thoughts and whose desire is for His people to know Him.

> For I desire mercy and not sacrifice, and the knowledge of God more than burnt offerings.
>
> —HOSEA 6:6

> But also for this very reason, giving all diligence, add to your faith virtue, to virtue knowledge . . .
>
> —2 PETER 1:5

The benefits of knowing God are essential to the well being of the Body of Christ. They are also essential to the building of His holy temple, a holy nation, that will reflect His glorious light.

> Grace and peace be multiplied to you in the knowledge of God and of Jesus our Lord, as His divine power has given to us all things that pertain to life and godliness, through the knowledge of Him who called us by glory and virtue.
>
> —2 PETER 1:2-3

> For it is the God who commanded light to shine in out of darkness, who has shone in our hearts to give the light of the knowledge of the glory of God in the face of Jesus Christ.
>
> —2 CORINTHIANS 4:6

By increasingly knowing Him, we partake more and more of His grace, peace, light and glory. In order to partake of His benefits, it is not enough, however, to know about God, but also to know Him in the sense of adhering to and having a personal encounter and relationship with Him. That holds true in our daily lives as far as our families, our communities and countries are concerned. Having studied about the United States didn't make me a citizen. I had to leave behind old acquaintances and places, cross a vast ocean, and learn a new language. I had to commit to and pledge allegiance to a new land in order to become a citizen and to appropriate new qualities, experiences and benefits as an American citizen. Similarly, our knowledge of and encounter with God requires a departure of our old thoughts and ways. Are we willing to forsake our carnal thoughts and immerse ourselves in the knowledge of Him who is holy and full of glory? What an extraordinary gift God has given us to have paid the price, by the death of His Son, to free us from our enslaved minds. He paid the ultimate price so we might be transformed by knowing Him who is holy and who is the God of knowledge.

> No one is holy like the Lord . . . Let no arrogance come
> from your mouth, for the Lord is the God of knowledge.
> —1 SAMUEL 2:2–3

What a gift of God it is to allow us to know Him and to become triumphant citizens of His kingdom which is unshakable and which endures forever. At the turn of a new millennium, in view of present day perils and uncertainties of the world's future, it is imperative for believers around the world to hunger for and to increase in the knowledge of God. No matter how volatile life on earth may become, God's purposes remain unmoved. His plans are for good and not for evil. Man has his own plan, but God has the final word.

> For the Lord of hosts has purposed, and who will annul
> it? His hand is stretched out, and who will turn it back?
> —ISAIAH 14:27

No matter how many onslaughts and trials the Body of Christ has yet to face, the kingdom of God triumphs and stands firm. Moreover, it will welcome and protect its citizens who, by the knowledge of and faith in the Lord Jesus Christ, have taken the journey ordained by God's grace from the kingdom of darkness to the kingdom of light. Those who are cleansed by the water of His Word and redeemed by God's grace, that is deeper than the ocean, will inherit all the benefits available to His citizens of triumph and grace.

> Now, therefore, you are no longer strangers and foreigners, but fellow citizens with the saints and members of the household of God.
>
> —EPHESIANS 2:19

As citizens triumphant in God's kingdom, let us be faithful with thanksgiving and praise to Christ our King. Let us allow Him to purify, restore, rule and reside in our hearts and minds as we increase in the knowledge of the Lord and become partakers of His eternal glory that shall cover the earth.

> For the earth will be filled with the knowledge of the glory of the Lord, as the waters cover the sea.
>
> —ISAIAH 11:9

To contact the author, write:

E. Von Bruck
P.O. Box 4222
Middletown, RI 02842
U.S.A.